Awakening the Divine Soul

Finding Your Life Purpose

Rosanna Ienco

First published by O Books, 2009
O Books is an imprint of John Hunt Publishing Ltd., The Bothy, Deershot Lodge, Park Lane, Ropley,
Hants, SO24 0BE, UK
office1@o-books.net
www.o-books.net

Distribution in:

UK and Europe
Orca Book Services
orders@orcabookservices.co.uk
Tel: 01202 665432 Fax: 01202 666219
Int. code (44)

USA and Canada
NBN
custserv@nbnbooks.com
Tel: 1 800 462 6420 Fax: 1 800 338 4550

Australia and New Zealand
Brumby Books
sales@brumbybooks.com.au
Tel: 61 3 9761 5535 Fax: 61 3 9761 7095

Far East (offices in Singapore, Thailand,
Hong Kong, Taiwan)
Pansing Distribution Pte Ltd
kemal@pansing.com
Tel: 65 6319 9939 Fax: 65 6462 5761

South Africa
Alternative Books
altbook@peterhyde.co.za
Tel: 021 555 4027 Fax: 021 447 1430

Text copyright Rosanna Ienco 2008

Design: Stuart Davies

ISBN: 978 1 84694 154 2

Printed by Digital Book Print

O Books operates a distinctive and ethical publishing philosophy in
all areas of its business, from its global network of authors to
production and worldwide distribution.
This book is produced on FSC certified stock, within ISO14001
standards. The printer plants sufficient trees each year through
the Woodland Trust to absorb the level of emitted carbon in
its production.

Awakening
the Divine Soul
Finding Your Life Purpose

Rosanna Ienco

BOOKS

Winchester, UK
Washington, USA

CONTENTS

Dedication

This book is dedicated to the memory of my dear angels:

Amanda Iredale—thank you for being the best friend I could ever ask for.

My beautiful niece, Lisa Ienco—thank you for all the lovely memories, I miss our laughter together.

I also dedicate this work to my father-in-law, Alan Barned, a wonderful dad and grandfather.

To my dear friend, Hardip Chopra, thanks for the many fun times we shared, you always made me smile.

To my precious children—my greatest teachers, Keanu, Aragorn and Amethyst. I thank you for choosing me as your mother in this lifetime. You each inspire me everyday with your glowing presence, reminding me of my true purpose. I deeply honor you all and our soul contracts.

To my husband, Andy, for your unconditional love and support and for understanding that a bird cannot be caged.

To my mother, Carmela, a real Goddess, who has taught me the true meaning of endurance—I honor you for your strength as a woman. It has given me the will to emulate this in my own life. Thank you for believing in me (despite what the doctors said when I was in your womb) and for knowing that I had a purpose to fulfill.

To my father, Guiseppe, for bringing me into existence and for helping me to grow as a person. Although we never knew each other, through my sadness I have found acceptance.

To all who have taught me how not to live, empowering me to use my wings of freedom.

To all of you who seek to find your own truth and purpose and desire to fulfill your life's mission. Embrace it with courage, strength and beauty.

To my teachers, guides and Power Animals, I honor and

respect you. Thank you for the grace and wisdom that you have shared with me, and continue to do so, throughout my life's journey. I am truly humble.

To all who dare to Dream...

Foreword

Rosanna's story, which you are about to follow, is a fairytale, a guidebook, and an invitation. I remember years ago when she first came on an introductory weekend course in shamanism, her bright eyes and enthusiasm. Little did I suspect that weekend was to be a mile marker in her life. Together with Mandy Iredale, her wonderful friend talked of in these pages, sadly no longer in the Land of the Living, she came on several more courses. But it was first several years later when she called me from England to tell me of her impending trip to Greenland in the depth of winter that I realized the depth of her commitment. I had lived in Greenland years before. "Why are you going to do that?" I asked. "They told me to on a shamanic journey," she replied. And so she went – and found out why!

There are many different ways to live life. Most of us try to choose what we feel is the "best way", the best way being influenced by many factors including our desires, worldly goods, what Aunt Martha will think, and many factors we're not even aware of. Some of us are pulled in another direction, looking for The Way, which is somehow qualitatively the *right way*. Some may call this "following your dream."

Some of us go a step further, becoming aware of the path which is laid out for us and following that path, no matter how challenging it may seem before – and after - the first step is taken. This is what Rosanna has done. She writes: " *If you have the courage to step outside of your comfort zone, then you will not only be amazed by the marvel and sights of the world, but also with the wonders that lay deep within yourself, acknowledging their spiritual beauty and the messages they hold.*" And then she generously shares with us the adventure her life is as she allows herself to be led by the messengers of the Universe.

But this is not a book of a boasting woman who has made it,

proclaiming "See how beautiful and pure I am!" No, Rosanna shares with us her doubts and misgivings as challenges meet her on her way. She gives gentle hints and encouraging exercises we can do when we ourselves are faced by what may seem to be overwhelming life obstacles. Yes, it's her story, but her message is that we can all do it.

If you are holding this book in your hand it is probably because you know your true path is just in front of you, but....

Turn the page – it may well be your first step into your real life.

Jonathan Horwitz
co-director of The Scandinavian Center for Shamanic Studies

Author's Note

This book and the exercises within are in no way a substitute for therapy or medical advice. If you have any medical conditions, seek the advice of a professional healthcare provider. The author is in no way responsible or liable for your actions, the manner in which you use the information contained herein, or the effects that may arise from performing the given exercises.

My personal, spiritual experiences, whilst in an altered state of awareness are not based on any real events or teachings from any indigenous cultures, but are described purely as they were shown to me during my own meditations and journeys.

Preface

When I was twenty-four years old, I ventured out into the world to find my true self. I left my hometown of Toronto for the glitter and glamour of Los Angeles, where I hung out with the rich and famous and attended music award shows. From there, I headed to London, England, where I pursued a career as a backing vocalist.

At first I thought I had found my calling, in the exciting world of the British pop scene—enjoying the parties and staying with a well-known musician friend, who lived in London. I did not realize, however, that this was not my own path—it was someone else's journey. Although my dreams appeared to be flourishing, this was not my destiny and it could not last—I had a rude awakening. I found myself with nowhere to live and only fifty pounds in my pocket. I had to make my way into unknown territory—I was alone in a strange city, facing an uncertain future. My dreams had dwindled and I was forced to focus on survival.

I got a job, working at a club in the heart of the city and I found a place to stay. My landlord lent me a book—*Going Within* by Shirley MacLaine.

As I read it, I looked at my life again and asked the question, 'Who am I and why am I here?'

My long search for self-healing and understanding had begun. Little did I know that I was jumping onboard the biggest roller coaster ride of my life, as I unearthed events, emotions and new perceptions. Everyone's life contains ups and downs, twists and turns, but it is our choices and how we chose to interpret the ride, that makes the difference.

I look back at the series of events in my life with a smile. I have survived the traumas, the disappointments and after all the struggles and the darkness that seemed endless... there still came an opening, like the first light of day, the first glimpse of the sun rising in the morning. It was in those very moments of deepest despair that I had my greatest awakening. I found an inner strength that I never thought possible. It took me many years to be able to fully trust myself and surrender to the unfolding of the Universe. Had I learned that lesson earlier, my journey of self-discovery would have been shorter, but then I would have missed out on many additional lessons offered by my spirit guides. When I did finally surrender, the most incredible inner peace entered my way of being. By sharing my teachings, meditations and Shamanic journeys, I hope to inspire you to attain that same degree of self-fulfillment.

During the process of putting this book together, many new and exciting adventures presented themselves. As I share with you the experiences of my life, hold on to your seats—if you really allow yourself inside your true essence and begin your own journey, it may just be the ride of your life! As you start to unearth your guides, your path and your purpose in the world, may you find contentment and as you awaken your spiritual core, may you be inspired enough to really open your eyes—to look at the world and your life through enhanced vision, so you can find out and truly understand why you are here. May you hear the deepest whispers of your soul. May your guides come and when they do, hold their hands and trust in the journeys they will take you on. This book may begin a new road for you, towards a more spiritual and fulfilling life. If that is what you desire, with all your heart, it will happen. Your guides will call to you and teach you what you need to know. No matter what situation you are in, or where you come from, there is always a new day and a fresh start. We all have the power to live our lives in peace, balance and harmony.

Come journey with me.

Rosanna Ienco

Introduction

For me, writing this book was the hardest thing that I have ever done, except perhaps for being a single parent. As I went through it, chapter-by-chapter, I had to face countless challenges. During the process of my own Divine Soul Awakening, I encountered many different situations and phenomenon that were necessary for my growth. This does not mean to say that your own awakening will be as challenging as mine was. Take from this book whatever you deem to be useful on the road to finding your life purpose and leave the rest behind.

I can recall when I was just nine years old and I received my very first diary for my birthday. I knew back then that this was the key to my purpose—to expand my imagination and to write. Somewhere along my path it got forgotten—I never thought that I could amount to something as grand as an author. I felt like the stupid girl for most of my life—afraid to speak my truth. Rooting from low self-esteem, I felt like I had no voice, resulting in a huge fear of public speaking that haunted me until only recently. I was so petrified at even the mere thought of it, that it prevented me from moving forward with my life. What I never forgot was how to dream—for if you forget how to dream... a part of the magic is lost. If there is one element in this book that awakens you—helps you to understand why you are here and remember those long forgotten dreams... then I have done the job right—fulfilled my mission. Go back to what you aspired to be when you were a child... bring it all back to life and make it happen. Keep your dreams alive and always believe in yourself.

Through the process of creating this book, I have truly learned that anything is possible. If you believe in it with all of your heart and soul... it will happen. After each chapter, I offer you short steps, keeping you in the moment and in the flow of that chapter. The exercises at the end of the book relate to each chapter, but are much more in-depth, allowing you to take your time to find the appropriate moment and fully expand with each exercise.

We all have choices in life—if we choose the road of self-growth, then we must be fully responsible in being committed to making the changes that are required. By searching to find your life's purpose, you are asking to hear messages from deep within your core. If you truly ask… then quite simply, you are ready. This book has been such a gift for me… a gift that I now offer to you—to assist you in unlocking your truth, finding yourself once again and understanding what deep down you already know—your life purpose. I share with you my own journey and how through many challenges and spiritual adventures, I finally found the key to my life. In doing so, I pray that this book opens your heart and takes you into the abyss of your essence. There is so much more to you than you have ever imagined. Are you ready to unveil your deepest mystery?

As you open the door to begin your new journey, may you be blessed with love, light and beauty. Thank you for sharing in my adventure and for journeying with me into the depths of my soul.

Inside each and every one of us is true brilliance.
It is deep down in your very core.
Capture the essence of your being and bring it into creation.
Explore and expand, to touch the world with your magnificence.

Rosanna Ienco

To believe in your spirit is to take a step of courage into the
unknown,
knowing that you have totally surrendered to the Universe.
To do this is to fulfill your soul's purpose.
It takes great courage and strength to embark on a journey
within,
for the inward journey is the core of your being and your truth.

This is my journey...

CHAPTER ONE

The Journey Begins ~ Understand Who You Are

Everything is silent, your life is at a standstill.
Clarity enters, your sight becomes brighter.
You are wiser, the lesson has been comprehended.

I could hear the pounding of the drum. As my heart began to race the beat grew louder. I found myself traveling rapidly through a long dark tunnel. Filled with curiosity and anticipation, I drifted forward, weightless to what seemed to be the lower world. I knew of this place from the descriptions I had heard and read about. I moved quickly through the passage, the opening of a powerful tree growing in the woodland. I named this tree my Grandmother Tree and I called her this because she is old and strong.

I started to giggle, I felt like an innocent girl playing freely in the green hills, amongst beautiful flowers with the soft wind blowing through my hair. The experience was beginning to remind me of when I was given laughing gas during childhood visits to the dentist.

The giddiness ebbed. The strange darkness of the passage had brought me to my destination, or so I thought. I heard the familiar sound of running water, which was very soothing and calming for me—I started to feel much more relaxed. I could hear the sweet melodies of birds singing and my fear began to evaporate. I had embarked on a journey and awakened part of my soul.

I came across a small pond and felt compelled to jump into the still clear water. I found myself swimming underneath, leaving the air and sunlight behind me.

I felt as though I was going between worlds, the lower and middle. I felt obliged again. This time I came up to the surface but

I was jolted backwards, discovering it was solid ice. I could not break through. I swam until, suddenly, I was met by a polar bear that had pierced the frozen barrier with the strength of his paw. I gently broke through the splintered ice and as my head popped up, I saw a new landscape.

This was a snowy white plateau surrounded by mountains, it was very cold but, curiously, this did not bother me. I looked up and I could see a brightly lit sky with hundreds of stars shining down on the spectacular scenery. I pulled myself out of the water and was immediately met by an Inuit man.

He had chocolate-brown eyes, short black hair, chiseled cheekbones and a wispy moustache. I guessed he was around forty years old and carried a great strength with him. He stood tall and I knew instinctively that not even the greatest wind force could knock him down. We looked into each other's eyes and he smiled warmly at me. There was something very familiar about this man, as if I had known him all my life. For the first time, I had met a spirit guide.

In the distance I could hear Arctic wolves howling. These mysterious sounds made me feel comfortable and welcomed by this beautifully barren landscape. In a strange way it felt like home.

I have always had an affinity with wolves. I believe the strength of these magical spirits can never be broken and I admire their continuous loyalty to the pack. I see the wolf as an important teacher; the wailing cry enlivens me and reminds me who I am.

My eyes started to fill with tears, as I felt that something very special was about to happen.

My new teacher kindly reached out his hand to gently take mine and led me inside an igloo. It was pleasantly small and cozy. Seated around the shimmering white walls a council of elders waited to greet us. Standing up as we entered, the two men and two women gazed affectionately at me, a wordless welcome in their eyes. Their faces were old and leathered—each line representing the wealth of knowledge and wisdom they had gained throughout their many years. An overwhelming feeling of love and strength washed over me, I felt safe.

We all sat down and formed a circle. To show my respect, I averted my eyes and looked down at the snowy ground.

'Do you know who we are?' asked one of the women.

'No,' I replied, softly.

'Do you remember when you were a young girl and you loved to make angels in the snow? Do you remember when you looked up to the sky—there was always a star, brightly shining down on you? That was us, we are your guardians.'

Tears filled my eyes and warm trickles of salty moisture rolled silently down my cheeks. Gratitude for their love fuelled my tears and the igloo was filled with warmth and love. One of the female elders placed a basket into her lap and took out a small silver fish. She passed it to me, indicating I should eat it. It was very salty and tasted very similar to mackerel. After I had my share I passed it to the woman who sat to my left. She had such an aura to her, mystical, that of a raven, so clever and powerful. This woman held the key to the gateway of the unknown. She ate a sliver of the fish and then passed it on.

After we all had eaten, I was handed a bundle wrapped in a colorful blanket. As I unwrapped the blanket, I had to catch my breath. Within was a fragile being, the most wondrous sight I had ever placed my eyes upon. It was a tiny baby boy! His eyes were sharp like a razor, his essence as peaceful as the pristine snow. As I held him there was an inner knowledge and bond between us that resonated deep in my heart. It was as if he was a part of me. I held this precious child so very close and was overwhelmed by joy. Tears, once more, began to roll down my face and that was the very moment when a storm of emotion came over me. I shuddered with excitement.

I felt a little confused as to the significance of this infant. Why had she presented me with this wonderful gift? The answer to this would be revealed to me later on in my life, but right there and then, I could only wonder in a warm silence. I continued to cuddle him, bringing his delicate body even closer, carefully embracing him with tremendous love—the kind of love that only a mother would feel for her own child. I was filled with awe as I observed him for a short while before placing him safely back into the arms of his guardian.

I was led back outside by the elders and taken to a small frozen lake. They guided and supported me across the slippery surface, as I made my way down through a hole in the ice that led to a fast flowing river. I slid into the water. As I dove down, I could see the lower world once again. I was surrounded by luscious green hills. The calling of the drum signaled that it was time to leave this exciting new experience and safely return to reality...

This was the very first Shamanic journey that I took on a workshop with Jonathan Horwitz, of The Scandinavian Center for Shamanic Studies. I can still remember it as clearly as if it was yesterday. It changed me and transformed the course of my life. It instilled in me a confidence in the unfolding of the Universe, a sense of being protected by my guardians and a desire to learn more and undertake further journeys.

When embarking on a Shamanic journey you enter non-ordinary reality by altering your state of consciousness with the guidance of a drum or other musical instruments. The rhythm will safely assist you to connect with your spirit helpers, to receive healing or guidance with issues in your daily life. There are different realms you can enter. Before moving into your entrance (which some describe as an opening in a tree, an animal hole in the earth or others have even entered through a cave), you state your intention and where you are going. For example: the lower world (this may be underground), the middle world (this may be a place that you can relate to in your physical world), or the upper world (some would describe as the sky, stars, clouds or the planets). Journeying can be very helpful to bring balance and

4

harmony into your life. We all have helpers in the spirit world who assist us on our life's journey. Some may come in the form of a human, others as animals (we would relate to these as our Power Animals), or any other form.

In the months to follow, I had many more visits to that arctic wilderness I relate to as the middle-world. Since I was a child, I have always had a profound connection to indigenous cultures throughout humanity. Therefore, it was not surprising that my guardians were manifested as members of another culture, one in which Shamanism had been practiced for generations. It was from my amazing experiences, during these most sacred journeys that the birth of my Inuit family would begin. Through my travels into this non-ordinary reality, my Inuit family would appear more frequently and the bond between us would become even stronger. Eventually, after various meetings, I was led to a potent, wonderful place that I call my physical, spirit home—majestic Greenland.

It is very important for people who practice Shamanism to build up a deep relationship with their helpers and the most crucial element has to be trust. I trusted what my teachers had been showing me and I headed to Greenland in search of a Shaman, despite being three months pregnant.

The word 'Shaman' was originated by the Tungus people of Siberia. In Michael Harner's book, *The Way of the Shaman*, he defines a Shaman as 'a man or woman who enters an altered state of consciousness—at will—to contact and utilize an ordinarily hidden reality in order to acquire knowledge, power, and to help other persons. The Shaman has a least one, and usually more, 'spirits' in his personal service.'

Shamanism dates back several thousands of years. A Shaman can be defined as a seer, medicine person or even a magician. Some were used to predict the weather. Others would heal a person by curing an illness or by extracting an intrusion from a patient's body. Many different people from all occupations now practice it. There are still many Shamans today, all over the world, who play various different roles in their society. When you enter the world of the Shaman, you embark upon a journey into the spirit world.

I could feel my body burning up as I started to digest the crystallized ginger I was nibbling on. This helped me with my nausea, as we were experiencing turbulence through the wind and snow. Finally, the six-passenger plane made it to the small community in Greenland. After a few days of searching, I was very fortunate to locate an old wise woman from the village, whose grandfather was the local Shaman. A local boy escorted me to her house. I sat down beside the woman; she smiled at me with curiosity as to why I had come to see her. I tried to explain, but she didn't speak much English. She offered me some tea, I smiled back at her feeling a little uncomfortable and wishing that I had an interpreter with me. I asked about her grandfather, the Angakoq (a word for Shaman), she must have understood because she pulled out a family photo album and graciously introduced me to her family through the pictures. By the time I finished my tea, I felt that it was time to go. The well-mannered old lady showed me to the door, smiling at me.

She declared in her broken English, 'You come back, you come back.'

Although disappointed, I knew that I would return someday.

That night, I received a call from the hotel manager, urging me to go outside and witness the delightful display. I swiftly put on my snowsuit and boots to hurry outside. To my utter enchantment, I saw the Aurora Borealis shimmering across the night sky. The lights were fluorescent green, swirling all around. I was told of a belief that an unborn child can see the incandescence from within the womb. I placed my hands tenderly on my belly, for the first time, after months of emotional turmoil, right there in the stillness of the night, I truly understood my purpose—my son. It was on this trip that I began unravelling the mystery of

Shamanism as it related to my life.

The next day I went back to England, vowing that one day I would return.

Have you ever been in a place where you felt totally connected? Somewhere you felt you were in harmony with, like a snowflake merging into the landscape. At times we need to take a leap of faith. To surrender and most importantly, live our truth as we know it. When we surrender, we are no longer fighting with ourselves; we then allow the natural rhythm within to flow. At times, it may be difficult to let go, causing more frustration. Therefore, have courage and trust in yourself because when you do, there will be a new opening for you, a new understanding. I am so grateful and feel very blessed to have encountered all of my experiences. Like planting a seed and watching its new life as it grows into a tree, my own growth has been endless. My life and how I see things would never be the same again. The journey within and without had begun. When I took this expedition to Greenland, the relationship with my helpers had only just started. Slowly the mystery would all fit together like the pieces of a puzzle and five years later, I found myself being drawn back to this magical place.

On arriving back in Greenland I set up another meeting with the wise woman, only this time I wanted to ask her to tell her own personal story. I arranged for a local Inuit woman, named Laila, to act as interpreter. She was very responsive and seemed happy to accompany me to the welcoming lady's home. We became well acquainted with one another as we strolled slowly but with purpose through the village. She was young and charming and spoke excellent English. We both enjoyed talking of other cultures and I discovered that, like me, she had a fascination and connection to Arizona and the Grand Canyon. I told her about my own spiritual experiences there and she expressed clearly that this was a place she would love to visit some day.

As we walked through the slush, fresh flakes began to settle.

The village would soon be covered in a blanket of snow. The landscape looked more breathtaking by the minute and I thought of how pretty the village would look at dusk, all lit up like a scene on a Christmas card. I have forever loved snow, as it has always had a healing effect on me—it gives me an incredible sense of peace. That may explain why so many of my journeys have taken me to snowy landscapes. At that moment, it reminded me of a time when I was a young girl growing up in Canada, I adored making angels in the snow, and how the falling flakes would touch my face as I looked up at the sky to dream with the stars. We walked down the steep hill until we reached the bottom. We had arrived.

Laila knocked on the door of the wooden house. I felt eager and at the same time a little nervous as it had been many years since our first meeting together.

'Come in,' said a deep voice.

Laila opened the door and asked me to follow inside. The wise woman greeted us and I presented her with a bag of assorted multi-colored beads that she had requested the first time we met. The old woman had a lovely warm smile and piercing dark eyes that told a story of their own. An aura of vigor surrounded her. I intuitively recognized this to be the strength of her grandfather, who had been a well-known hunter and Shaman, back in the days when this was intrinsic to Inuit life.

We sat down comfortably in the middle of her living room to begin our conversation, but this time she was not alone.

There was a friendly, jolly old man with her, whom I was very pleased to meet. He referred to himself as 'the visitor' and he had a deep 'inner peace'. He was very enthusiastic and eager to join in with us. The cheerful man explained that he was a good friend of her deceased husband.

They both chuckled to one another as we began. She started to tell me how different life is now to when she was growing up:

'In my early years there were many Shamans,' she explained.

8

'Everybody knew of one. It has all changed now and people are quiet about it. There is still talk, but only in whispers.'

She then spoke of her father, a priest, who at the age of ten was one of the first in his village to be christened. He would tell her stories of her grandfather.

'How did your grandfather become a Shaman?' I asked her.

'It requires many years of learning in order to become a Shaman,' she said, reflectively. 'It takes as long as going to university. My grandfather studied!'

Then I asked: 'How was one chosen to become a Shaman back then? Was it handed down through the family?'

'Sometimes it was like that,' she replied. 'On the other hand, if a boy or girl were without parents, they would go seeking help to make a connection with the spirit world.'

She was adamant to illustrate how Shamanism and magic are completely different things.

She went on to say, 'For one to become a skilled Shaman you need to comprehend and have a good knowledge of both.'

She had an air of seriousness, as she explained how the apprentice needs to find an equal balance between the two.

'If you do not perceive both, there is a risk of becoming ill,' she said. 'And if you show signs of fear then your powers will go.'

The visitor pleasantly interrupted us as he sniggered to himself. The room was filled with cheer and laughter. He had waited patiently for his turn and now it was his time to join in with a story. He began to tell us of his hunting days:

'I used to go out with the kayaks,' he said.

There was a stern look on his face as he continued, 'One day there were three kayaks and we all went out looking to hunt. Suddenly, I spotted a polar bear!'

He was very proud of that and I could hear the elation in his voice as if he was reliving the experience all over again.

'This was a scary moment for me,' he said. 'I have only come across two polar bears in my entire life.'

His expression turned to fear as he went on with his tale, 'We did not shoot it right away because it was very large and too heavy to carry. We had to divert the bear towards the land before we could cut it. This was our way of life. We would also have to hunt many different kinds of seal, either by kayak or on the ice. The blubber was our only source of heat. Before we had guns, our ancestors would use spears.'

The old lady smiled as he finished reminiscing. She began to tell us more about her father. I asked her if he had ever wanted to continue the teachings his dad had been given.

'It was forbidden to practice the old ways when my father was growing up,' she said, firmly. 'You had to tell all of your secrets and knowledge of Shamanism to the priest. Once this was done and you had revealed everything, you would then have to be christened. You were not allowed to speak of it anymore and no one was permitted to carry out the old traditions.'

There was a look of sadness in her eyes as she related this to me.

'Do you know of any Shamans who still practice now?' I enquired.

She laughed to herself.

'No not really,' she replied. 'Society has been split into two parts. In my opinion, once you become christened the old ways can no longer be used.'

I asked if she knew about any of her grandfather's experiences.

'He practiced Shamanism all the time,' she said. 'Then one day, he was calling out to his helpers and guardians. The spirits that he hailed upon kept saying, "I cannot see your wife and child anymore." Later that same day, when his family returned home, he found out that they had just been christened.'

The old woman looked very grave.

'After that day he never practiced Shamanism again,' she announced. 'Instead, he too became a Christian and began to read the bible.'

I felt a sense of despondency to hear how it had all suddenly come to an end. When the old woman was a child, she remembered many of her relatives asking Shamans for help when they were sick.

'They would sometimes get well and not be sick anymore,' she said. 'It depended on how good or powerful the Shaman was.'

'Do you believe that someone can still become a Shaman today?' I asked.

'The old ways are gone,' she replied. 'Back then there were no other traditions or religions to worry about. We did not know the rest of the world. I believe that it worked back then, but now everything has changed. In my opinion it is not powerful anymore.'

Our conversation was coming to a close. I finished by asking her what she sees in the future for the younger generation.

'They are going to live it as it is now,' she replied. 'Everything has turned into another culture. They will continue to have a new lifestyle. I am very fortunate to have been raised with the old ways and traditions,' she added, with a dignity that conveyed her commitment to remembering her people's past.

She will continue to carry the knowledge with her. The proud look on her face said it all.

I felt honored to have witnessed these anecdotes. I said goodbye to this intriguing lady and the sprightly old man and thanked them both for sharing their stories with me.

I gave them each a hug and gathered my things. The visitor started to clap his hands in excitement to show his appreciation. I was very touched by this. His cheerful smile will never be forgotten.

Laila and I climbed up the steep hill. The snow was still falling, even heavier now than before. I was enjoying the walk. Laila headed back towards her house. I thanked her for her time and wished her well. Eventually I reached the top of the hill. I stopped to look out over this gorgeous, picturesque village, pondering what I had just heard and watching the snow falling all around me. I started to absorb all that I had encountered here in Greenland. I thought of how significant and how profoundly accurate my journeys had been. It all made sense to me now, my life and my spiritual path. It was amazing how there had always been a meaning to everything I had done. I contemplated the wise woman's stories. A moment of bleakness came over me when I realized how different things would be if they were still living the old ways, rich in culture. I then reflected on the expansion and development I had observed within my friends and myself since we first started to practice Shamanism. I realized that Shamanism has not been lost.

I looked back at all the lessons I had endured and begun to appreciate. The fascinating experiences I have been so fortunate to encounter. I could not imagine my life without applying these ancient ways. Through Shamanism I have developed a strong connection to the spirit world that relates to certain events that happened to me in my physical reality. It was my Shamanic journeys that encouraged me to visit Greenland, to bring together all the pieces of my life steadfastly assembled by my teachers. In Greenland I found a sacred and serene land that mirrored my many journeys.

I had a feeling of renewal on my return. A tower of strength stands tall within me. I was ready for the next chapter of my life, but that mystical place often comes back to my mind. I miss the land that is so special and sacred to me, and the serenity I felt from the mountains—so peaceful and yet so potent. I especially loved watching the mist creeping mysteriously across them and the Northern Lights dancing in the sky like green streamers, illuminating the upper atmosphere. The radiant smiles of Inuit people and the laughter of their children, playing in the village instilled warmth in me as I was carried across the wilderness by a pack of huskies. For many villagers this is the only means of travel during the harsh winter months.

I am very grateful to these alluring Arctic sledge dogs for making my adventure complete. The howling, as they called to one another in the night, was pleasantly haunting. It was humorous and uplifting to watch them play together—affectionate one moment and fighting for authority the next. I learnt a great deal from observing their behavior.

My Shamanic journey merged into one with my reality—forever fixing Greenland in my mind as the real-life embodiment of my middle world. I was amazed how often we underestimated the power of nature and all it has to offer. I truly believed in those moments of oneness that nature is our greatest teacher.

The essence of this land has lingered on inside me. It has become my home of inspiration because for a place, so cold, I had never felt such warmth. I went on this journey in search of finding a Shaman and understanding why my teachers had led me there. What I had found instead was a piece of me that I did not know existed. The deep calling inside me was awakening to a sense of understanding and belonging. The depth of my soul was now starting to be unveiled as, layer by layer, my truth and my purpose, were being revealed—like a snake shedding its skin.

My new teachers in the spirit world, my guides were there to carry me through the lessons and adventures of this thing we call life. I knew then, that we all have them guiding and working with us on our life's journey.

Step One to Finding Your Life Purpose ~ Surrender

Now take a moment for introspection. Be silent, close your eyes and take a deep breath, visualize a peaceful setting. Take a moment to ask your inner self, what would your middle world look like? Notice the landscape, is it day or night? What can you hear? What can you smell? How does this place make you feel? Breathe in this serene scene, knowing that you are safe. Ask yourself, where do I deeply want to be at this moment in my life? Take another deep breath, surrender in truth—your truth. Let your soul talk to you and let your spirit guide you—understanding all that you are.

CHAPTER TWO

Clarity Through Silence

Walk in strength, know your destination.
Stand tall, be your truth.

I awoke to the yelping of foxes in my garden—the cries sounded like a newly born baby waiting to be cradled in its mother's arms. I looked out of my bedroom window and saw a precious sight. Two auburn coated foxes were standing face-to-face, rubbing noses like they were kissing. I felt as if I had front row seats to a private movie premiere, which was for my eyes only. I thought for a moment, I was still dreaming, I continued to watch—filled with admiration, as these two ardent foxes were clearly courting.

'There is more to this,' I murmured.

I could feel the altered state of awareness shifting my sense of reality. (As a student, one of the lessons I have learned on my spiritual path, is to stay alert to the messages from above, which do not always come at a time of my choosing. Sometimes messages can be a sign of something to come and they may begin from a real life experience. As you attune to your own soul journey, you will learn to recognize the lessons that are being sent from the Universe.) I looked over at the clock—it read 5:05 am. I must have been very tired, as I immediately fell straight into a deep sleep, where upon, I had a vivid dream.

I dreamed of a strong and handsome Native American man. He was tall and powerful, with very prominent facial features. He looked as though his ancestors came from the Southwest, perhaps Arizona or New Mexico. His aura was calm and cooling, like a free-flowing waterfall on a hot summer day, yet within his tranquil essence, there was also a magnificent warrior spirit. I could not help but feel an attraction towards this intoxicating man. His long, silky, black hair was especially appealing to me.

'Who are you?' I asked.

There was no reply. He looked right into my eyes, as if he was staring directly at my soul. I knew this man on some mysterious inner level. As I returned his gaze, I could feel my heart chakra expanding and the connection between us grew even stronger, enveloping me in a wave of jubilation.

The clock read 8:28 am—it was a lovely bright morning. I looked out of the window again, but the foxes were gone—leaving behind a trail of litter from a garbage container they had knocked over. Inspired by my dream, I began thinking of the trip I had planned to the United States—there were so many things to organize. I was off work for the summer and had been invited to a Sun Dance in Nebraska. I would also be traveling to a few other parts of America that held spiritual significance for me. Although I was not leaving for about a month, I decided to start getting organized. Then completely out of the blue, my friend, Nicole, called me with an amazing suggestion—a week-long trip to Egypt. She had found a bargain flight that left in five days. As crazy as it seemed, we both decided that it was too good a deal to pass up and besides, I had always dreamed of visiting the pyramids. By the end of the day, our travel arrangements were completed.

Five days later, I found myself on the plane, drifting off to sleep and into a dream state. One of my spirit guides came through to speak with me. His image was a little blurry, but his voice was easy to understand.

'Be strong,' he said. 'I am here to protect you on your path.'

The vision was getting clearer and I was taken to a little spirit baby—the one that was shown to me in my very first Shamanic journey. The infant was still with his guardians. One of the elders passed him to me and I held him tenderly in my arms. I felt even more connected to this sweet boy and I knew we were bonding once more. We began to dance and I held him so close, wrapped up in a blanket of motherly-love. It was as though our body rhythms were flowing naturally into one another, just as a stream flows freely and endlessly into a river. We looked meaningfully into each other's dark eyes and smiled—expressing only the purest adoration.

I took him to an inviting ocean where a dolphin was waiting for us. I gently placed this precious child into the warm water to frolic with the friendly dolphin. The calming waves were azure blue with splashes of aquamarine. Quite unexpectedly, the dolphin vanished and an enormous whale appeared from nowhere. I gasped in wonder, as it brushed softly against the infant, as if bestowing a kiss. The baby giggled, reaching his tiny fingers to touch the sleek fin of the Orca. When the reveling was over, with one flick of his massive tail, this gentle giant slid back under the waves from whence it came. As I reached over to pick up the contented child, I noticed two timber wolves approaching along the beach, their huge paws leaving deep impressions in the soft sand—they had come to escort the beautiful boy back to his spirit home.

I opened my eyes, blinking a little at the brightness of the cabin lights. I immediately reached for my journal to record the details of this moving vision. As you begin your own soul journeys, it is always a good idea to have a notepad handy, because just like dreams, your recollections of them, usually fade fast. By immediately writing them down, you preserve the information to reflect upon at a later time, when it might be more relevant. It could be hours, days, weeks, months or even years before the meaning becomes clear. Your logbooks will become an important reference, as the significance of your soul journeys gradually unfold.

During a meditation I had taken before we left England, my spirit guides told me that this trip to Egypt would open up my brow chakra (my third eye) and that it would help me to see things more clearly. I was also there to heal a past life issue that would present itself. Nicole and I settled into our hotel and after resting briefly, we ventured out for the day. The searing and relentless heat would normally have been unbearable, but I was almost oblivious to it—I was feeling so euphoric to actually be in Egypt, visiting the great pyramids. I decided to take a camel ride to make our journey to the great pyramids even more exciting.

Nicole, on the other hand, declared, 'I shall not go near such a mountain of a beast.'

She was disgusted by the way it constantly broke wind and made weird slurping groaning noises, whilst grinding its teeth together. Instead she rode a well-mannered, white horse. Nicole is a captivating young woman, always attracting the attention of men with her jovial but firm presence—especially so in Egypt, because of her long, straight blonde hair and big, baby blue eyes. Her idea of 'slumming it' would be staying at the Hilton—she does enjoy her life of luxury! We seemed to gather crowds of men wherever we went, which proved to be somewhat of an annoyance. On our way through the town, beads of perspiration trickled down the inside of my top and as my body heat began to rise, I could feel my cheeks turning ruby red.

I kept smiling to myself, as I was so grateful for the chance to connect with this historical site. It was strange because on some unknown level, I felt as if I had been here before. It seemed so delightfully familiar to me. I gave thanks to God for bringing me here and for the wonderful opportunity that had unexpectedly presented itself.

As we wandered from village to village, on our way towards the pyramids, we received smiles from some of the curious and warm-hearted people, but others just stared and there were some that would not even look at us.

The blistering heat became even more intolerable, but mercifully we came across some young boys selling ice-cold cans of pop. I do not usually indulge myself with sweet carbonated drinks, however, on this occasion, I decided I would definitely enjoy some. I could have drunk just about anything to quench my raging thirst. (It turned out, the particular part of Egypt we were in on that day, was one of the hottest places in the world.) After our refreshments, we continued on with our journey and it was not much longer before we had our first glimpse—I could make out an image of the pyramids in the distance. In that moment, I had a strong feeling of eagerness. There they were, standing right before my eyes. I took a deep breath accompanied by a big sigh of relief. I had waited a very long time to see this spectacular view. I have always been fascinated with this mysterious place, but up until now, I had only seen photographs in books, which did not do it justice. I was totally in awe of the power and majesty of this ancient land.

The archaic monuments were very busy and overcrowded—there was a multitude of tourists visiting from all over the world. I could feel the potent energy of the site—there was an intensity almost beyond description. I believe anyone would have felt it, just being in the presence of such an electrifying place. Especially drawn towards the Sphinx, I was very fortunate to escape the tourists and spent a good time there in solitude. Legend claims that when the Sphinx was buried in sand, visitors would seek wisdom from its lips.

Back at our hotel that night, I kept waking up in cold sweats. I was having anxiety attacks and they were so severe, I felt like I was going to die—right there in Egypt. Every time I fell back to sleep, I would be woken up by the same recurring and horrific dream. I could see only darkness and I felt something or someone trying to hold me down.

I heard a woman's voice chanting over and over again, 'You are going to die, you are going to die.'

In an extraordinary way, a piece of me actually was dying. I believe that as we grow and learn, a part of us dies each time we release the things that no longer serve us purpose. We let go of the old to allow the new to enter—like a butterfly emerging from a chrysalis.

Our rational mind can sometimes stop the flow of energy that leads to such possibilities of new doors opening for us. If we do not stay open to the opportunities that came our way, we can become trapped by illusions, habit or obligation and like a fly entangled in a spider's web, many people find it impossible to free themselves. If you have the courage to step outside of your comfort zone, then you will not only be amazed by the marvel and sights of the world, but also with the wonders that lay deep within yourself, acknowledging their spiritual beauty and the messages they hold.

The next morning we had a very close call on a horse and buggy ride. We were traveling through the town when a car suddenly headed straight towards us. The brave horse instinctively veered off to the side of the road, rescuing us from this reckless driver and only narrowly avoiding running into a parked vehicle. We were so thankful, as this courageous animal put its own life at risk to save ours.

The last few days of our visit I spent reflecting on my time in Egypt. There is so much more to life than we see—the magic, the mystery and the beauty. The incident with the horse awakened another part of myself—made me think of how preciously short our lives here on earth really are and how important it is to live the best life that you can.

My final night in Egypt, just before going to bed, I took a Shamanic journey to one of my guides and asked to connect with my past life here in Egypt. I put on my headphones (so as not to disturb Nicole, who was fast asleep) and listened to my drumming CD that helps me shift my consciousness into the necessary state. I mentally affirmed my desire to link with my past life in Egypt and then my journey began.

I made my way to the middle world—this time it was a dry desert where a gray-haired old lady was waiting for me. She was very elderly (I guessed around ninety), with cavernous eyes, which made me terrified to look at her. She approached me and tenderly wrapped a black cloth around me.

'It is not yet time for you to have the knowledge of your previous connection here,' she said. 'I am here to clean out your third eye, so that you may see more clearly.'

Without any warning, the wind gusted, tugging at the cloth. I saw a misted haze and realized a sand storm was on its way. I was now feeling a little anxious. I was even more uncomfortable when she transformed several times into a skeleton.

'We will all look like this one day,' she told me, before resuming her human form.

She reached out her arms to touch my face with her wrinkled, bony hands.

'Don't be scared of me, I am here to help and heal you,' she explained.

The old lady caringly placed a clear crystal ball into the center of my brow, gently stimulating my third eye. As she did so the gale died down. She looked at me and smiled.

'You are here to assist others,' she said.

Once again, she dramatically turned into a skeleton, before vanishing. I came out of the journey feeling heavy and drained. The gift of having my third eye cleared reminded me that there is so much more to life than we see through our physical eyes. We need to be alert, follow our instincts and listen to our soul.

The next morning, Nicole and I caught a flight back home, but there was no time for me to relax, as I had to prepare for a Shamanic training course I was attending the following day. I spent the weekend of the course undertaking more Shamanic journeys. I always enjoy taking journeys—connecting to the spirit world comes naturally to me. This is my comfort zone, altering my state of consciousness and finding a balance of awareness between the two worlds.

I chose to walk this path long ago and I knew when I made the undertaking, it would not be easy. I was aware there would be many fears to face, especially my inner demons. I believe that we must first rid ourselves of any pain or phobias, before we can really feel and appreciate full spiritual bliss. I know it is attainable by all of us, because I experienced some incredible journeys that weekend—here is one of them:

I immediately went to my Grandmother Tree. I stood there and waited patiently for a guide to greet me. After a few minutes, a large black bat appeared before me. He thrashed his wings indicating for me to follow him. I grabbed hold of him tightly, as he took me to the upper world. We were ascending higher and higher into the cloudy sky. I looked down, but we were so high up, I could no longer see the land. My body was feeling much lighter, like I was going through an initiation—one of re-birth. We continued to fly rapidly through the clouds. I saw a shade of cerulean blue travel through me and at the same time, I had a sensation of exhilaration.

As we descended back towards my Grandmother Tree, I noticed a graceful snow-white swan, waiting for me at the edge of a lake. She was stunningly beautiful and stood so proud. She gazed right at me, communicating with her eyes—as if speaking words to me. She quickly faded and was replaced by a gorgeous, pure white mare, which had a noble magnificence. I climbed onto her back and we galloped at great speed, through the passage of the tree, until we ended up in the lower world.

She led me to a cave, where I carefully dismounted and walked towards the entrance. As I went into the cavern, the walls sparkled with precious amethyst crystals. I ventured further inside and sat in the center of this immensely healing chamber. I closed my eyes, inviting the therapeutic powers of the Amethyst to cleanse my body. The gleaming phosphorescence was radiating through my entire being, starting at my feet then working its way up to my head and back down again. My body felt totally rejuvenated—I was calm and ready for the next stage of my life.

This Shamanic journey was preparing me for my outer

journey—the summer holiday I had planned to the United States. The bat represented rebirth, which was very significant for me at that point in my life. The swan taught me of grace and the amethyst gave me the healing and cleansing that I required before this vacation, but I remained blissfully unaware that this trip would change my life forever.

My Shamanic journeys were growing stronger and clearer. I felt honored and humbled that I had such a loyal and formidable team of Power Animals and spirit teachers that were guiding me in my life. There I was, on the verge of something so sacred and I was ready to evolve—my spiritual path was about to expand.

After a long flight and a total of nearly ten hours traveling, I finally arrived in Nebraska. My friend, Samantha and her husband picked me up from the airport and drove me to their home, where I would be staying. I was so exhausted. I went straight to bed and immediately fell into a deep sleep.

The next morning, we headed to the grounds, which were being made ready for the purification ceremony, in preparation for the Sun Dance. I was waiting with anticipation for my best friend Mandy, who had arranged to meet us there in a few days. Samantha and I decided to take a stroll along the river. On the ground in front of us, she noticed a soft, brownish owl feather.

She picked it up and said, 'I think this is for you.'

She tried placing the feather into my hands but, much to her surprise, I would not take it. Although a part of me wanted to, my fear was overriding the urge to accept the gift. (I have always thought of the owl as an omen of death which, at the time, scared me).

'Thank you,' I said. 'But it is obviously meant for you, because of your strong connection with owls.'

Mandy arrived just one day before the Sun Dance was due to begin. She had flown over from England to join us. It was a relief to have my best friend with me. I missed her and was starting to feel anxious about being there. I was experiencing strong emotions and having powerful dreams. Mandy and I always confided in one another, sharing our Shamanic experiences together. She had a special way of understanding me, even when others could not. The energy felt much lighter now—she was able to relax the atmosphere with her energetic presence and her warm smile, which matched her heart. Sharing the same tent together, I saw a different side of her that I had never seen before. This other side was a very humorous one—she had the exceptional ability to make me laugh out loud. After arriving, many emotions started to surface for her too. We sat by the river and shared our feelings. Later on, we joined in with the other women, who were gathering sage in the fields. It was our first time witnessing such a sacred dance. We were deeply honored and thrilled to be able to support Samantha, her husband and the rest of the sun dancers. We even had the incredible privilege of witnessing the medicine man being made chief.

This amazing experience touched our hearts, transforming Mandy and I forever. It taught us of sacredness and how important it is in life to honor others. We are all unique and with so many different cultures, we may not always understand or agree with other people's traditions, but we should respect their beliefs, as we are all individuals here on this earth.

That evening, after the dancing and ceremonies had finished, we all sat around the warm glowing campfire and reminisced over the events of the last few days. I was a little sad that the Sun Dance was over, but I was looking forward to the drive we had planned through to Arizona. Just before returning to my tent, I noticed something bright against the darkened night sky. It was a shooting star streaking across the heavens—the first one I had seen for many years. My whole face lit up as, somewhere deep inside of me, I knew that something extraordinary was coming my way. I quickly made my wish—to meet my soul mate very soon.

We traveled through Colorado and New Mexico, enjoying the spectacular scenery along the way and then eventually we arrived at the Grand Canyon. A series of in-depth journeys and meditations had led me here. My teachers had told me that this was my spirit home (another significant place like Greenland that truly touched and guided my essence). The first few nights that we camped at the canyon, I had powerful dreams at night, in which I repeatedly saw my feet being planted into the earth and felt the nurturing and love of the great mother.

One morning, I decided to take a Shamanic journey (I found it very comforting to journey in my tent, whist lying down on the ground). I could hear the heartbeat of Mother Earth beating through my body and resonating with my soul.

A man appeared to me, riding on a large sturdy bison. I was overcome with emotion, because I recognized him as my soul mate, or twin flame. We had waited a very long time to see each other and I could not hold back the tears as they seeped out onto my cheeks. I heard a voice.

'Listen to the night owls, they will guide you.'

My heart started racing and I rapidly came out of the journey. I was left wondering about the significance of the owls.

After lunch, I decided to go to the visitor's center to have a look around. I was casually admiring the exquisite Native American crafts in the gift shop, when something jumped out at me. I had glanced at a picture of a waterfall in a very sacred place and everything in my being, knew I had a strong connection there.

'That's it,' I said softly. 'I have to go there.'

The next morning I said goodbye to my friends and set out on my own. I was quite nervous, as I had never camped out by myself before. Under the guidance of my teachers, I threw myself into the unknown and surrendered, trusting that the universe would protect me.

The hike down to the sacred waterfall was arduous, but adventurous. When I reached the bottom of the canyon, I made my way towards the campsite, but with another four miles still to go, my feet were already aching, the sun was scorching and I could feel a blister forming on my toe. Just then, I could hear singing coming from right behind me. I turned around to see a young man with short blonde hair, blue eyes and a growth of stubble on his chin. As he caught up with me, he introduced himself as Lawn and offered to carry my backpack for me. He had already set up his tent, arriving three days before we met and he planned to stay for another four. He was on his way back to the campsite after having a bite to eat in the local café—nestled in the village amongst the canyon walls. At that point I was extremely exhausted and, looking into his eyes, I did not believe he would run off with my pack, so I graciously accepted. In return, I agreed to pay for his next meal in the café. He was so delighted that he wanted to give me a gift. Lawn stopped at the side of the trail and took out three feathers from the pocket of his denim jacket. 'There you go,' he said, as he handed them to me. 'I found these in California and I would like you to have them.'

I looked at these amazingly significant feathers and laughed out loud. 'I don't believe this!' I exclaimed in amazement. 'Owl feathers!' I remembered back to the Sun Dance, when Samantha wanted me to have the owl feather that I rejected. This time, I felt that I should have the feathers, as an owl spirit was obviously guiding me on my adventure. I politely accepted, leaving behind any superstition that I once believed.

When we reached the campsite, I said goodbye to Lawn and set up my tent beside a stretch of the river that I called 'my heavenly blue lagoon'. It was now dusk. I sat by the stream and felt like I had found my home. I began to cry, as I looked at the red canyon walls, the trees and the gentle flowing river. I could not believe I was in this unimaginably pretty place. My soul knew this location in a way that I could not describe. That night, before I fell asleep, I sensed the presence of the man I had dreamed about, the morning I saw the foxes in my garden. His spirit appeared to me in my tent. I could feel his black silky hair on my body, his tender touch on my face. A rainstorm of bliss started to move through my soul. 'This is crazy,' I thought to myself. 'This man doesn't even exist. Who is he?' I opened the flap of my tent to look outside. It was dark except for the alluring moon shining down— almost full. Attempting to unravel the mystery, I started to think about my trip to the States and the people I had met. I thought about growing up in Toronto, how different I was back then, never leaving the house without wearing stylish clothes and cosmetics. I was now lying in a tent, with no makeup or jewellery, hiking boots, blistered feet, black shorts and a sweaty tank top. I felt so at one with nature, as if I was bearing my soul to the earth.

'Why was I really here?' I pondered.

I had been guided so perfectly by my intuition, Power Animals and spirit guides. After being around musicians and working in London nightclubs, I had been shown a very different side to life that was very new to me. This place was alive with natural beauty—it was real. Until now, I had been fooled and confused about what was authentic and what was just part of the facade. It took my pilgrimage to this serene place for me to see the difference.

Do you know what is genuine in your own life? It can be difficult to tell when you are caught up in the rat race of life. At times we need a different routine, or a new atmosphere. Ask yourself this—are you ready for change?

It was sunrise—I could hear the dawn chorus of birds chirping to one another. I crawled out of my tent, stretched my arms and dug into a 'power bar' for some nourishment. It was a perfect morning to go exploring and experience more of this breath-taking landscape. It was not long before I came across Lawn hiking down the trail. I arranged to meet him at ten o'clock in the café, to buy him breakfast.

Two miles further along the path I noticed a dark and intriguing cave set back against the wall of the ravine. I wanted to investigate but my foot was really sore, so I sat on a rock and removed my hiking boot and sock to check the throbbing blister.

'Are you alright?' I heard a man's voice call out to me as he approached.

'I have a nasty blister,' I replied.

'Oh, that looks like it requires attention. Do you have anything to burst it with?' he asked.

'No, I don't. I left my first aid kit in my tent,' I explained.

'Hang on, I'll get you something. My tent is just over here,' he said.

The kind man told me his name was Curry. He was in his forties, he wore glasses, had short curly hair and a warm, friendly smile. I felt there was a bond between us—he could have easily been my brother in a previous lifetime. Curry was here camping with some friends. He returned with his first aid kit and treated my blister. I thanked him and arranged to join up with him a little later, as they were hiking to one of the waterfalls.

The 'power bar' that I had eaten earlier was wearing off and I was starting to feel quite hungry, so I set out for the café to meet Lawn for breakfast. The cool air was very refreshing at that time of morning. I wanted to take advantage of this and hike the four miles to the village and back before it became too hot.

On my way there, I saw a baby fox hiding in a crack in the chasm wall. It stared right into my eyes. It reminded me of that morning I was woken up, mesmerized by the two foxes courting. I was getting used to my daily hikes—I did not want to leave this tranquil heaven. The thought of going back to the noise, the cars and the pollution was just too much for me to bear right now. The reality was that I had to leave sometime, but this ancient place was now a part of me and I was a part of it—we were one. It was beyond the surface, deeply rooted within my soul, which understood everything about this land. My core was navigating my whole trip. It is truly amazing how different our lives are when we allow situations to flow naturally, like the cascading waterfall, and permit the Universe to steer our course.

I met Lawn at the café and bought him breakfast, as promised. We enjoyed our meal together—I remember how wonderful the herbal tea and toast tasted and I watched with interest, as many locals and tourists came in and out. It was now late morning, so I said goodbye to Lawn and made my way outside. I walked around the village for a short while to become more familiar with my surroundings and then decided to head back to the campsite. The thought of bathing under the waterfall was becoming very inviting, as I had stayed longer than I planned to and I could now feel the full torridness of the sun's rays. It was at that moment that I saw a man heading towards me. He was an extremely good-looking Native American man in his early thirties, with a calm but mystical aura. He was very tall—around six feet—and he had beautiful, long, silky black hair. His broad shoulders and massive chest were signs of the warrior spirit that he carried with him.

'Oh my Goodness, it's him,' I murmured.

He looked exactly like the man in my dream. We both looked at each other and smiled.

'Hi, how're you doing?' he asked.

My heart was beating so quickly, I could hardly get the words out.

'I'm d...doing great' I stuttered. 'How 'bout you?'

'Good,' he replied. 'I was thinking of going for a swim later, would you like to join me?'

'Sure,' I said, trying to stay calm (the resemblance of this man to the one in my vision was freaking me out).

'My name's Damon, what's yours,' he asked.

'Rosanna, I replied.'

We shook hands and looked at each other curiously. I thought of how foolish I must be, going swimming with a complete stranger, but on a deeper level, he wasn't a stranger at all—my soul had recognized him the moment I looked through his eyes.

'Meet me back here at around five o'clock,' he said. 'I've got some things to take care of until then.'

We said our goodbyes and parted ways.

The hike back seemed to take no time at all, probably because I had been focusing all my thoughts and energy on this mysterious man I had just met. I could not get him out of my mind and the more I thought about him, the more the butterflies multiplied in my stomach, so I knew that the attraction must be a powerful one. I snuggled down in my comfy spot under a tree, overlooking the soothing stream. I tried not to analyze the situation too much, as it made me nervous. Instead, I allowed the tranquility of the flowing water to calm me.

Have you ever met someone and known immediately that you were connected—some kind of inner awareness that you cannot describe? Have you ever had a meeting with another soul, which was so profound it transformed your life forever? I just knew there was a bigger picture—one that was beyond my comprehension. Souls don't lie—I trusted my heart.

It was five o'clock and there he was, looking so strong and handsome. We smiled at one another as we walked towards the waterfall. This particular one was more secluded than some of the others, but still just as magnificent. It felt like a secret place, veiled by the many trees that blocked the view of the canyon. There was no one else around—we had it all to ourselves. I was so relieved to remove my hiking boots and finally go swimming. We both disrobed, leaving just our swimsuits. Damon took my hand and helped me step into the cascading spray. I lowered myself leisurely into the surprisingly cold, but very refreshing, blue, green water and began to swim. He dived in to join me. It was as if we were both being cleansed before beginning a sacred ritual.

After a short while, he called me over to where he was swimming and at this point I felt a little vulnerable. I was getting apprehensive, but he reassured me by telling me all about the waterfall and about himself. I then shared with him my own story of my life in England. He looked a little surprised when I told him I was camping out by myself. We swam for an hour and then he invited me to have dinner at his house. I gratefully accepted, thinking how nice it would be to have something to eat other than 'power bars' and peanut butter and jelly sandwiches.

His home was small and cozy. We ate some delicious tacos and then listened to music. We both had similar tastes—like me, he was a huge 'Led Zeppelin' and 'Pink Floyd' fan. He moved closer to me and, in that moment, my body began to tremble, as we were attracted towards each other like two magnets. He too started to shake, as we held hands and looked into each other's eyes.

'Wow!' he exclaimed. 'This energy between us is freaky.'

'Yes, I know what you mean,' I whispered.

We went outside to admire the stars. He put his arms around me and we embraced one another fervently. I held him so close to me and I wanted to cry. This sea of emotion had created a tidal wave inside of me from previous lifetimes together. Right there and then, I knew he was the man in my dream—the man whose spirit came to visit me the first night I put up my tent. I could feel it in my heart and soul—it really was him! The man in my journeys, the one my teachers told me about—the man on the buffalo!

I was overwhelmed by all of this and as we stood there in the warm evening air, we were even blessed by the radiance of a full moon. This was a serious encounter—he was my twin flame. He looked at me, respectfully acknowledging that this was a meeting of two old souls, who had come together again after many lifetimes apart.

The weather changed suddenly. The wind picked up and storm clouds covered the moon. It became very chilly outside, so we decided to go back into the house. It would have been difficult for me to walk back to the campsite in darkness, so I agreed to stay until morning. I was very happy with this decision, as it meant I could get to know him better. We spent the night together, enveloped in each other's aura, linking our energies and recognizing our deeper connection. The more I looked into his eyes, the more I would remember about our past existence here together. It came as short flashes, almost as if I was watching a slide show of our lives. We were so in love—a love that was pure.

From nowhere, I felt a deep, piercing pain in my heart, like an old open wound was, at last, being healed. Bizarrely and yet beautifully, this meeting with my twin flame was both agonizing and at the same time, enormously euphoric.

Eventually, morning came and it was time for me to hike back to my tent. I only had a few more days before I was to due to depart this heavenly place. As for Damon and I, we agreed to keep in touch and planned to meet again in a month or so and take a trip together. Our union was not at an end—it was just the beginning of our sacred contract together.

Step Two to Finding Your Life Purpose ~ Acceptance

Now take a moment for introspection. Be silent, close your eyes, and take a deep breath. Think of an attribute that no longer serves you. Now release it as if you are peeling away a part of yourself— lovingly let it go with love and light, allowing something new to enter. Do you detect any fear within your being? Accept the fear— truly acknowledge what it is you are fearful of. Now bravely embrace your fear and lovingly let it go. Breathe in the new energy—allow it to flow through your entire body.

CHAPTER THREE

Run No More ~ The Mirror Shatters

There will be a time when there is no more running,
the mirror holds the truth.
Your truth is your freedom, know it, be it, walk it, live it.

For some people, the inward journey is not an easy one and it was no different for me. I reached a point in my life where I had more questions than answers. I found that even on my darkest days the tide would come in for me, revealing answers, but it always flowed out again too, leaving me a little confused. However, I also discovered that the wind always blew me in the right direction. In those moments of murkiness, as hard as it was at the time, I gave thanks for each desperate moment, because in those painful places, I eventually found my brightest glow and my greatest enlightenment. Sometimes it is the deepest cut that can reveal to you, the very core of your flame. It is in these moments when you can see the blessings that come from within. That is when you can appreciate what you are surrounded by. At times, it takes a little soul searching to touch your truth and to fully understand these blessings.

After a grueling flight from England, I arrived at Phoenix airport. I still had a two-hour bus ride before I made it to Flagstaff. I was to meet Damon the next day. We had kept in touch by telephone, but we had not seen each other in over two months and I couldn't wait to be with him again. When I finally arrived at the hotel, I put my luggage away and casually looked over at the window. I was startled to see a huge raven perched on the ledge outside, staring back at me with eyes as dark as the night. Then with a flap of its wide wings, it was gone.

'Wow!' I yelled, 'That was an intriguing experience. It's good to have another helper with me.'

It reminded me of a dream I had a few years ago, when a raven greeted me. In my vision I was holding the raven close, when I looked into its piercing, black eyes, I felt myself traveling through a tunnel, as if I was journeying into the very eyes of the raven. The raven symbolized a gateway into the unknown and the sighting of a raven at my window was very auspicious. I was feeling very sleepy, so I had a light dinner and headed straight for bed. I felt a little apprehensive about seeing Damon again. I wondered if he still looked the same.

Early that morning, there was a knock at the door. I took a deep breath and slowly opened the door. It was Damon, standing tall wearing jeans and a burgundy shirt. He looked even more handsome. His prominent features stood out even more with his black, long hair tied back. At first, we just stared at each other, and then our nervousness dissipated. We embraced one another. This time I was not trembling and neither was he. We were thrilled to be in each other's arms again. We spent a blissful day together in the town, getting re-acquainted. That evening we went out for a romantic meal and then on to a club where we laughed and danced—lost in our own euphoric world.

We continued on to the hotel where we rekindled our passion. I had a powerful dream about a baby bluebird. It nestled at my ear to sing me a sweet, melodic song. It was so vibrant a blue, it reminded me of the blue lagoon where I swam with Damon that summer. When I woke up, all I could think about was the precious spirit child in my Shamanic journeys. 'Was there a connection here?' I thought to myself. I told Damon about the dream of the bluebird and he said it was a beautiful omen of something good to come.

The next day, we headed for Las Vegas with the crazy notion of getting married. We both had a great time there, but a problem arose that would eventually separate us and prevent us from being together—our cultural differences. As much as I wanted to fit into his Native American culture, one that I deeply honor and respect, I was not a part of it and his family was never going to accept me into their lives. The daydream of a chapel wedding had faded into the ether. We tried not to discuss the matter any further, making the best of our remaining days together. Our time in Las Vegas had come to an end. Our drive back to Flagstaff was awkward. We both knew that we had to say goodbye and in our sadness we hardly spoke. Our energies were quite low, so we stopped at the side of the road to rest a while. Looking into each other's eyes, we said very little. We both agreed that our situation seemed much bigger than either of us.

'I need some time out to think things through,' he said.

My stomach dropped, as if I had just plummeted from a precipice.

I glanced behind me and saw the most breath-taking sunset I had ever laid my eyes upon. We both sensed that it was very mystical. The color of the sky was, fiery red, blaze orange, and deep purple, melting together into a heavenly haze. I felt a subtle shift inside of me and I had an inner knowing that there would always be a bond between us — we were twin flames.

A whisper in the wind spoke to me, 'You have both created something incredible — you have a new life inside of you.'

I have never felt such serenity, as I did in that very moment. I was very blessed to have that sacred encounter.

Damon drove me to the airport, I was uncertain if we would ever meet again. It was immensely difficult for me to say goodbye to him, as I had fallen profoundly in love with this man — our souls were connected forever.

Many months went by and we hadn't been in touch with one another. I accepted the fact that I would never see him again. I looked down at my belly, it had grown bigger and I could no longer tie my own shoelaces. My beautiful baby boy, as I knew him to be, was a calm energy. He slept a lot and did not move around in my womb too often.

I had a pleasant pregnancy, despite all the emotional turmoil I went through, before I accepted that I would be a single mother. I found an inner strength that I have never had before. It may be that I inherited this from my mother, because as a single mom of five, she was the pillar of strength in our family and it is her blood that runs through my veins.

After many journeys, bonding with my spirit boy, I would soon be able to hold him in reality. I looked forward to the years ahead when we would travel together on our sacred journey as mother and son.

When I went into labor I was fortunate to have the support of my friends, Andy, Nicole and Mandy, who helped me through it. Andy set up my birthing pool for me, (I had been instructed in a dream by one of Keanu's ancestors, that it was important for him to be born surrounded by water) and five hours later, Keanu was born naturally in the water. He took his first breath outside of the womb, looked at me with a gentle pout and then released his first naked cry into the world. I held him close to my body and gave thanks that the baby I held in so many of my journeys had finally arrived. As we looked at one another, tears of joy rolled down my face as I sobbed from my heart and soul. From that moment on, I knew that my life would never be the same.

Living in England as a single mother was not easy and had its challenges. I had to think seriously about how I would support the two of us, as savings were staring to dwindle.

I could not bear going back into the stale and smoky atmosphere of the nightclub, and besides, my champagne drinking days were over.

I started to have exciting Shamanic journeys that took me to Hawaii. It is interesting that I gave my son, Keanu, a Hawaiian name (meaning, cool breeze over the mountains), it is the perfect name for him, as in his innocence he was still pure in spirit.

I always listened to the guidance of my teachers, as I knew from past experiences that they always led me to the right place for the right reason, even if the road to enlightenment was not always blissful. After being on the spiritual path, I had finally crashed down heavily into harsh reality. Not only with the challenges of being a single parent but my inner demons were starting to surface and sometimes I diverted from my spiritual direction. We have all experienced some kind of challenge or another in our lives. When life feels difficult and you feel that the challenge is too great to be met, remember that it is all part of your journey, your growth as an individual, as a soul who has come here to gain knowledge and to grow. Have courage and continue to walk your truth. Surrender into it and see it as a blessing.

I followed the guidance of my spirit guides and I took the destined trip to Hawaii. (My best friend trusted me enough to lend me the money knowing that I would return it as soon as I could, which of course, I did.) Keanu was only nine months old and I did not know at the time that this would be my most difficult quest so far. I had no idea of how far into the depths of my own darkness I could fall. This would be a voyage that would test my endurance.

Malia is a beautiful voluptuous Native Hawaiian woman with an inviting smile. Her heart so warm, you could see the sincerity through her eyes as she spoke. Her cousin, a friend of mine, suggested that we meet because of our similar spiritual beliefs. Malia met Keanu and I at Molokai airport and drove us to our apartment. During our stay in Hawaii, Malia and I spent a great deal of time together. She shared her knowledge and taught me the intricacies of her native tradition. When Keanu was asleep, we spent long hours undertaking Shamanic journeys. The spirits of this ancient land made their presence known to me. The first few nights I felt them taunting me. I have heard stories of people going mad on this Island, so I told Malia what I was experiencing and she advised me to call upon the spirits and talk with them. She then gave me a special gray stone for me to keep in my room.

Her spirit guardians had instructed her to give it to me for protection. We were told to place it into the ocean before we left Molokai. A few days later, the spirits finally allowed me into their realm. They began to nurture me and I felt at peace—the healing could begin.

I did so much crying during my time in this sacred place, I left behind my own ocean of sorrow. My Shamanic journeys were taking me deep within myself. At times, I felt claustrophobic—I could feel my deeply rooted pain surfacing. I wanted to run, but was trapped here by my inner demons, glaring back at me out of a giant mirror. I was forced to take a good look at myself—I did not know which direction to follow. I could not go back to working in a nightclub, so what was my purpose? What was I to do now? All of these things were haunting me.

Have you ever searched inside of yourself to ask what your purpose is? Do you believe there is a bigger picture, that God has a plan for you—that deep down you have grand plans for yourself? Are you ready to take the voyage into the core of your true self?

I had to let go of the person I saw in the mirror and my long held beliefs that I acknowledged were no longer valid. I had so much hurt inside of me—I had to let it all go before it consumed me. The truth was that I felt so let down and all alone. I had never felt that vacant before.

Layer by layer, I had to shed much of my old skin. One evening, I dreamed of being buried alive, my favorite flowers, purple orchids, were all around me. I saw my flesh being eaten by maggots until I was reduced to a skeleton. My body had perished but my essence was alive.

In the morning I felt like I had been reborn. I had let go of all the pain that was preventing me from moving ahead. My sad, angry and negative emotions had created my own turbulent sea, but instead of drowning in it, I chose to swim.

The intensity of my time in Molokai was a blessing. I

underwent a death and rebirth, while my precious son, Keanu, enjoyed playing with other children and experienced dolphins for the first time. I must have left behind the equivalent of three suitcases full of emotional baggage that no longer served me. On our way to the airport, Malia gave me a book of her cultural heritage. She told me there was something important inside it. When I opened the book, I saw a Pueo feather (the white owl of Hawaii). I was so honored that I hugged her. I thanked my friend (who I now considered my sister) for all of her support and guidance and for sharing her wisdom and culture with me. The gift of the owl feather reminded me of my sacred journey.

Our return flight from Hawaii suffered long delays, so the airline offered us half price tickets to anywhere in the South Pacific. Nine months later, I decided to go to Fiji and the Cook Islands.

When we arrived in Fiji, we checked into a hotel right on the oceanfront—it was paradise. Keanu was now eighteen months. We had so much fun together, we even hiked to a sacred waterfall and Keanu freely jumped into it. It was not at all surprising with him being a water baby.

After a couple of days, we took a boat ride to one of the smaller Islands. I had arranged for us to stay in a cozy hut on a fabulous white sandy beach, surrounded by dramatic cliffs. There were many backpackers there, who sniggered when they saw me dragging all of my luggage and a stroller along the beach. They must have thought I was completely crazy, traveling with my toddler to such a remote island.

The Fijian children loved having Keanu in their village. One child in particular took an interest in my son and he especially enjoyed singing to Keanu during his daily nap in the hammock. That same child rescued us from a potentially perilous situation. A huge centipede had crawled into our hut. Later, I heard that its sting inflicts agonizing pain on its victim, which can last for several days. The villagers believe that the only cure is to remain drunk for days, until the pain subsides. I considered us extremely fortunate and was very grateful to the brave boy.

One evening, we were invited to a Yaqona (Kava) ceremony at the chief's hut. I felt honored to be invited to this ritual. I brought with me some clothes and toys for the village children. According to legend, Yaqona originates from the Fijian God, Degei—whose name translates as 'from heaven to the soil and through the earth.' It is a turbid liquid, which is served in a large wooden bowl and drunk from a half coconut shell. It is customary to drink it all down in one go. Sharing a bowl of Kava is said to create an invisible bond between the partakers.

When it was my turn, I politely accepted, clapped my hands once, said, 'Bula' (which means hello) and began to drink from the coconut shell. There was an unusual tingling and numbing sensation on my tongue. I also discovered that it had a very strange flavor—quite peppery. I prayed that I could down it all without regurgitating, as that would have been disrespectful. Thankfully, I managed to drink it all without heaving. I passed on the cup and clapped my hands three times. Yaqona is non-alcoholic and is neither a stimulant, nor a depressant, but it had a calming effect on me which was somewhere in the middle.

When the ceremony was finished, I went over to say goodbye to the chief. He invited Keanu and I to his home the next day for lunch and I graciously accepted. We made our way back to our hut and listening to the hypnotic sound of the ocean crashing against the rocks, we fell asleep.

The next morning, after breakfast, we spent time on the beach making sand castles. We had so much fun that our bodies were completely covered in sand. We went back to the hut to get ready to go to the chief's home for lunch. I finished bathing Keanu and turned around to grab a towel but when I looked back, I realized, to my horror, that the door was wide open and Keanu had run out of the hut.

'Keanu, where are you?' I shouted in a panic-stricken voice.

'Oh my goodness!' I exclaimed. There he was, naked in the middle of a field, where several of the village men were playing soccer. All that I could see was a bare-bottomed toddler, streaking all over the pitch. Thankfully, the men found it humorous, which helped to make my blushing cheeks return to their normal hue. That moment remains etched on my mind. As embarrassing as it was, at the same time it was hysterically comical.

We arrived at the chief's hut and the entire family was there, waiting to greet us. They all sat on the floor cross-legged where there was food laid out on top of a brown colored cloth. We sat down and enjoyed the delicacies of chicken, fish and yam. We especially liked the coconut milk that was pleasingly refreshing. We all got to know each other quite well. I was surprised by the interest his two sons were taking in me.

I was even more perplexed when the chief looked me right in the eyes and said quite emphatically, 'Why don't you and your son stay here? We can provide for you both, especially as I have two sons with whom you can choose to marry.'

I started to blush once again.

'Thank you,' I replied. 'But I need to get back to England, I have people waiting there for me.'

(I didn't really, but I needed to come up with an excuse. The truth is, my friends were busy working and life was proving to be very lonely for both of us. I knew that I needed to change our lives, but as much as I loved this island, it would have been far too drastic a change and besides, I was concerned about Keanu's future.)

'Think about it,' said the chief slowly. 'The opportunity is open for you.'

The next morning we took a boat back to the main island and checked into a hotel for a couple of nights, before our flight to the Cook Islands. I didn't feel at all well. I was getting worried that something I had eaten at the previous day's luncheon, had not agreed with me. Fortunately, Keanu was fine, but that night, while he was asleep, I was violently ill—I have never experienced so much purging before in my life. I felt as though I was being initiated into some kind of brutal, flushing-out ritual. All through the night, I was contemplating going to the hospital.

Thankfully, the continuous retching ended the next morning, otherwise I don't know how I would have managed to take care of Keanu. Between the Kava ceremony and lunch at the chief's hut, my physical, mental and emotional body had undergone a spiritual transformation of healing and cleansing in preparation for new things to come.

Our body knows when we are on overload. Like an engine, it could not keep running without an oil change, so how can we expect our own bodies to? We endure so much stress in our society. When you hold so much emotional and mental baggage, it needs to be emptied in order for you to live healthily, otherwise you will feel heavy and lifeless. I think it is important for all of us to be in touch with our bodies. What are we putting into them and why? Be aware of what you eat, how do certain things make you feel? Do certain foods trigger off different emotions?

The experience that I had, made me become more aware of my own body and what it was telling me. As horrid as that incident was for me, my body was very grateful for the clean.

We left Fiji and stopped off in the Cook Islands for a few days. Everything was so pretty and colorful, reminding me of the beauty that we all have within. Sometimes, we choose not to see the beauty in all things, especially when we are going through challenging times. We tend to focus on our faults and the things that we don't like about ourselves. Instead, we need to see that our bodies are sacred temples, filled with buds ready to blossom into beautiful flowers.

We arrived back home, I made the decision that it was time to leave England and move back to Toronto, Canada. I put out the prayers to the universe and asked for it to happen. There was nothing to keep us here anymore, except for a handful of good friends, but I had to think of what was best for Keanu at that time. I thought it would be best for him to be close to my own family in Canada. I knew that we would both miss Andy, because although I had broken off our engagement five years earlier, we had kept a good relationship over the years and we had become close again. Andy was there with me to see Keanu into the world. He cut his umbilical cord, so there would always be a close bond between them. However, it was time to move on.

Keanu and I settled into our basement apartment in Toronto. I was not happy in our new dwelling, it was dark and cold, but I knew that it was only temporary, until we found somewhere better. I was feeling intensely lonely and I was missing my British friends, because there was no one in Toronto that I could really connect to, spiritually. I also knew that I needed to take a look at some of the more serious issues in my life. My personal insecurities that I held from when I was a child were creeping up on me. I had not realized just how much my childhood had affected me and how some of my relationships had scarred me, so I found myself having to look within once more. Sometimes the road to self-healing can feel endless, but thankfully we have teachers, helpers to guide us along the way. Although we may feel alone, there is always a hand reaching out to us in some form or another.

My mother did a wonderful job raising my four siblings and myself, having to be both mother and father to us. However, there was still that emptiness of not having a father in my life that has never left me. A huge part of me just wanted to know what it would be like to have a dad—that other parent to turn to for advice, or just to feel safely snug in his protective arms. Then there followed a pattern of abuse in my relationships. At the time it did not feel like abuse, but when I later stepped back from the situations to see more clearly, that is exactly what hindsight shows as the truth. We can easily be blinded and fall into a pattern of abuse, attracting one bad relationship after another. I believe that it can continue over and over again, until we actually deal with the cause by going straight to the root.

I found myself falling into a deep depression, but while Keanu was in day-care, I went back to college to further my education. I was training at the 'Academy for Learning' in computers. I walked about two hours each day, often in harsh weather, to get my son to day-care and myself to school and then back home again. It was hard and I felt very isolated. I had serious regrets about moving back.

To my surprise, my friend, Bruce from England, called me. He was touring the States for a few months before heading back to the UK and he had made friends with a Native American man in Oregon. He invited us to visit him and meet his friend. A few days later, Keanu and I hopped on a flight to Oregon and met with Bruce.

I was grateful for a change of environment and was glad to see Bruce and his friend Arthur. Bruce is a tall slim fellow and has the ability to make you laugh with his English sense of humor. His friend, Arthur, is a well-built, righteous man, who had much to teach us through sharing his stories of his life. He was working very hard to get his health back to par, as he was injured while serving his country in Germany. Arthur invited us to his hometown in Northern California. We were there just in time for a special celebration—'The White Deer Skin Dance.' This is a sacred dance amongst the Hoopa people that is dedicated to world renewal, accompanied by feasting and celebration. I felt very honored to be invited.

On our drive to Hoopa Valley we stopped off at Redwoods. What a potent place—we even spotted a bear. I immediately felt connected to the land. Keanu loved the enormous trees. We were standing in front of one of these old giants to have our photo taken, when a beautiful, light blue colored butterfly landed on my arm. When the sunlight caught its wings, it shimmered with a gorgeous array of different shades and tones. As we began to walk away from the tree, I could not believe that it rested on my arm, lightly clinging to me. I have never experienced anything quite like it before. A woman noticed and she could not believe it either. We were all amazed until the fragile butterfly eventually fluttered off of my arm but then continued to follow me, frolicking in the air around my head and shoulders. It was an amazing experience. I felt so blessed, as if a fairy was dancing with my spirit.

We finally arrived in Hoopa where we stayed with Arthur's mother, a well-respected elder named Minnie. She was a lovely woman, so very gracious—her big heart beamed through her welcoming smile. I really took a shine to her. We got to know one another quite well throughout that weekend. She shared wonderful stories with me about her life and her tradition. I confided in her about my life and the challenges I faced as a single mother and she kindly offered me some advice.

Bruce and I were highly privileged to witness the 'Deer Skin Dance' and I was especially pleased to see Keanu so joyful, playing with the other children.

Sadly, the time came for us to leave and so we went back to Minnie's house and packed our things. Minnie asked me to follow her.

'I have a gift for you,' she said.

I could not believe my eyes when she handed me a stunning butterfly necklace, with an Amethyst in the center of it. Amethyst has always been my favorite crystal and it has brought me much healing. The butterfly reminded me of my experience with my 'fairy' in the Redwood forest. I gave her an affectionate hug, after which, she also gave me a key chain with a traditional Hoopa amulet hanging from it. I keep it close by me as a special reminder of my significant time with her and her son, Arthur. I will never forget her—she will remain forever in my heart.

On the way back to Oregon, we all witnessed another sign of Nature's encouragement, when five deer crossed in front of our car. What a magical week it had been. I felt alive again, as the

'Deer Skin Dance' represented renewal. I re-evaluated my own situation once more and addressed some of the changes I wanted to implement.

The time that Bruce and I spent with Arthur had taught us about humor and how to live our lives in a righteous manner. I learned a great deal. As for my dear friend Bruce, I have been forever grateful for the phone call that he made to me on that lonely and desolate evening. I doubt if he has ever realized the enormously important role that he played in lifting me out of my unhappiness with his kind invitation.

There are so many blessings that surround us in our lives. I believe that the people we meet are sent to us for a reason, there is always a purpose—to help and guide each other in one way or another. Think of the people in your life that touch your heart and the ones that helped you in a time of need. Be grateful and give thanks to them and the blessings that they have brought you. You are never alone on your journey in life.

There are many tomorrows yet to come—the sun will shine, the rain will fall and no matter how long the road ahead seems to be, there are many more lessons and blessings along the way to where we want to be.

Step Three to Finding your Life Purpose ~ Blessings

Now take a moment for introspection. Be silent, close your eyes and take a deep breath. Give thanks for everything that you have gone through in your life, even the darkest moments of despair. What did you learn from those moments? Are there any emotions that you feel are buried somewhere inside of you, which need to be released? Ask yourself if you are ready to let them go. If you are, ask gently that you may release them with love and light. Remind yourself of the beauty that is all around you, and then breathe in this beauty. Find the blessings in each and every situation that you encounter.

CHAPTER FOUR

Animal Wisdom ~ Discover Your Power Animals

We are all like a burning fire, the little particles
of our essence, intertwined into a burning flame.

The aroma of wood burning in the distance tickled my nose. I looked up at the sky to see the smoke mysteriously merging into the clouds. This was a sign for me to prepare for this new experience. I would be entering a sweat lodge for the first time — a kind of ceremonial sauna, used for prayer and healing. I was a little worried that, once inside, I might panic because of my mild claustrophobia. My heart was racing like horses galloping in a derby. I wondered to myself, 'Why am I here in the middle of a field out in the English countryside?'

I could see everyone had already formed a circle. I found myself an inviting spot and waited patiently with the others.

The leader of the ceremony was ready to begin. He was a Native American elder. His hair was long and black with traces of gray. He had hypnotic eyes that stared directly into mine and I felt shivers go down my spine as he continued to glare at me.

I felt an attraction to this man — like a magnet; it was pulling me closer and closer towards him. At the same time, in my mind's eye, I saw a gorgeous, gray timber wolf. She stood boldly, but had a weary look on her face. She was facing the gate towards the exit of the field, as if she was showing me the way out. Not fully understanding, I did not heed this warning.

One by one, we were asked to enter the lodge. I was last to step inside — he gestured for me to sit next to him beside the entrance. The flap was closed; the only light was the glow of the red-hot stones that sat in the center of the hut. The leader poured water

47

on the stones and steam began to fill the lodge. I could smell the pleasant fragrance of sage, cedar and sweet grass as it was sprinkled onto the steaming stones. My body began to tremble, as my anxiety heightened. I felt the space diminishing and started to panic. 'Get me out of here,' I wanted to scream. The elder instinctively sensed my fear and held my hand. This calmed me down and I began to take deep breaths to control my anxiety attack. The heat was becoming unbearable, but instead of resisting, I surrendered. At that moment, my life-long fear of enclosed spaces vanished. The healing ambiance of the lodge, combined with the prayers that were shared, brought me a healing peace that showered my body.

Throughout the weekend, this man had taken a strong interest in me, so much so, that at the end of it, he asked me to be his apprentice. In awe of it all and at the time, still very naïve, I accepted. As I traveled around different parts of England that week with the group, I began to feel a little dizzy and out of balance. Strange things were happening to me. I saw so many different animals and my dreams were full of them. I told the elder about these animals because I was worried; so much was happening all at once, that I simply could not comprehend. He said he would protect me and take the animals away, so they would no longer scare me. The elder told me to embrace him and to breathe that animal out of my body as I exhaled. As I did this, he took a deep breath in and asked me to name them, one by one. I began to feel nauseous and very dizzy again. He held me so tightly, I felt as if I was being strangled. I started to cry in the confusion of it all. It was then that he told me about Atlantis and a past life that we had there with each other. He continued to describe how all of us, who were gathered in his group, were all reconnecting again from our lives together in Atlantis. At that time, I was not aware of having a previous life in Atlantis and I was starting to feel powerless and more scared.

I decided to phone home to check my voice mail. My mother

had left five messages begging me to call her, as she was worried and was having strange dreams about me. The last message said, 'Please come back home before it is too late.' Apparently she was having dreams telling her to save me.

My mother, Carmela, a warm caring woman, was born and raised in a small town in Southern Italy. With the biggest heart, she would do anything to help someone in need. My mother was the kind of mom that all my friends adopted as their own and I admire her courage in raising my four siblings and I single-handily. There has always been a deep spiritual connection between us, as if we are twin souls and we both always know when something is not right with the other.

All I could think of was the beautiful wolf, I had seen during the ceremony, and how connected we were.

The group was invited to a druid celebration where we were able to camp out on the land. That night, in the dreamtime, I had a very vivid vision. My friend, the wolf, came to visit me. We played together and formed a strong bond; we rubbed noses and I cuddled her. It was such a joyful dream that I did not want to wake up until, suddenly, a fierce, black wolf with bright amber eyes came charging at my wolf and viciously attacked her! I woke up in a sweat with my heart pounding. 'This was a warning,' I thought to myself.

I finally realized what I had allowed myself to become involved in and I knew that I had to get away before it was too late. I was acutely aware that I had spent several days entranced by this devious man's spell. All the while, he had been attempting to get closer, deliberately trying to weaken me by taking away the protection of my Power Animals. The very next day he told me I had been chosen to be wife number nine. Now I really knew things were dreadfully wrong. With the help of my Power Animal, my wolf, I was able to see the situation clearer and I could finally break free. I told him that I needed to go home, but would rejoin them a few days later. Thankfully he believed me and I escaped from his clutches.

Power Animals are dear, wonderful teachers. I believe that we all have them guiding us and, from time to time, they will enter our lives for several different reasons. My wolf came to warn and protect me that night and, many years later, she is still with me. I have various other animals that I work with and they too, have assisted me with different situations in my life.

Have you ever been drawn to a particular animal and wondered why? Did you ever think that this might have been your guardian angel in the form of an animal? Power Animals have appeared in many forms. In fact, any living creature can be your guardian spirit helper. I believe that our animal helpers appear to help empower us, by offering their love, beauty and protection. They also come to teach the lessons that we need to know. I continue to learn much from these amazing teachers. When you make that connection with your Power Animal, the teachings are between you and your guide. For example, if you have an eagle appear to you, then that eagle has come to you at that particular time to work with you, help you and guide you through your life.

Connecting with your Power Animals can be achieved through Shamanic journeying, through meditation or even by invoking them through song and dance. I have successfully used all of these techniques, but the one that I use regularly to consult with my Power Animals is Shamanic journeying. I use the method that Michael Harner explains in his book, *The way of the Shaman.*

My own experiences with Power Animals are always very influential—they are my teachers, protectors and friends. I am so grateful for them. If you choose to embrace the teachings, then a close personal relationship will form between you and your guide. We are truly unique individuals so our experiences will vary from person to person. I might have a particular Power Animal work with me when I need courage and then a different one with me when I need to see a situation more clearly. My wolf came to me to give me strength and to warn me of the danger I was in, to help me escape before I was harmed both physically and energetically.

A dear friend of mine, who had struggled with an eating disorder for most of her life, spent years trying different therapies and found that this was the only technique that worked for her. Through her journeying and building a trusting relationship with her Power Animal, she was finally able to overcome this huge obstacle.

Another touching story is of my best friend, who was in the hospital, dying of cancer. It was so heartbreaking to see the pain that she was suffering during her final days. I sat at her bedside and shared in her joy and her love for her magnificent Power Animal that had so beautifully, changed her life. The incredible connection that she had to this Power Animal, brought to her happiness and tranquility, whilst she lay in the hospital bed, in a great deal of discomfort. That was the last time I ever saw my friend. A couple of days later, she drifted into the heavens. I felt like a part of me had gone with her.

During the time Keanu and I spent back in Toronto, I had my own health scare. A lymph node in my neck was starting to grow and I was sent to the hospital for an ultrasound. The lymph node was a strange shape, so they decided to book me in to have it removed and checked, just in case it was cancerous. I was petrified, so I tried to put it at the back of my mind. I just focused on my son and the joy and love that he has brought into my life. I knew that we had a purpose in this life, a sacred path that we would walk together and I wasn't going to let him down.

One day, the week before my surgery, I took a nap with Keanu. I had a remarkable dream of the most striking, snowy owl. She glided towards me and a gentle breeze began to blow as she landed elegantly on my left shoulder. Calming snowflakes fell softly all around.

I looked her straight in the eyes and asked her, 'Am I going to die?'

The wind got stronger but I did not have any difficulty keeping my balance. In that very moment, I was no longer afraid. The snowy owl was still perched on my shoulder as I started to walk in a westerly direction. Her presence was so very strong that, when I woke up, I knew she was still with me and I felt she had come to tell me that everything was going to be all right.

I had my surgery and my owl was correct, everything was clear with my biopsy. She still remains with me to this very day. I feel so very blessed to have all of these incredible animals that work with me. I honor and respect them dearly. You too have Power Animals that protect and guide you. Are you curious to know what animals surround you? Be open to ask for their guidance, you may be pleasantly surprised with what appears before you.

I remember the time I was working in London, I wanted to leave my job but I didn't have the courage to do so. One of my Power Animals guided me and gave me the confidence to finally leave the job behind, as it was time to move into a new direction. How many times have we stayed in a situation for the fear of change? We get used to a way of life or a routine. You find that sometimes it is too scary to move forward into a new direction. If we don't take the chance to find out what's out there waiting for us, then how can we move forward? Is your life calling for a change?

After my operation, my life started to quickly change. Andy, my ex fiancé, came to visit Keanu and I in Canada. Our relationship was still strong and we were missing one another. After his visit, we began to email each other more frequently — we were still very much in love. A short time later, he asked us both to move back to England to be with him. Another phase in my life came to an end and I was ready to move on to the next chapter. Andy and I finally got married. I once heard a tale about the person who cuts the umbilical cord at birth—they are forever bonded with that child. I suppose there was truth in that as Andy and Keanu were now father and son.

Empowering Journey with Power Animals

We all have moments of inspiration and amazement in our lives. During the years of connecting with my Power Animals, I have experienced and witnessed some incredible moments. One time that I will never forget demonstrates the amazing connection that children have with their Power Animals. It is a perfect example of the beauty and healing that can come into your life. We were in Las Vegas and decided to take Keanu to the funfair at 'Circus Circus.' He was so excited to go on the rides; it was all he was talking about. As soon as we arrived, Keanu started to feel ill; he was a little dizzy with an upset stomach. I asked him if there was anything that I could do to help, but he just told me that he needed ten minutes or so, to sit on the bench quietly. I was feeling disappointed for him, as I knew how much he had looked forward to coming. Ten minutes went by and Keanu got off of the bench with a huge smile on his face.

I asked him, 'Are you alright now?'

'Yes, I am feeling much better now that my bear and dolphin came to heal me,' he said. 'My bear clawed the unpleasantness out of my tummy and then my dolphin took me swimming with her in the healing waters,' he added.

He looked totally different after that and we all enjoyed a happy outing.

When Keanu and I moved back to the UK to be with Andy, our new lives had started and we slowly settled in. Keanu started going to a local playgroup and I worked for Andy's company. I was happy to be back and to be together as a family, but I still had that deep calling of purpose that I couldn't quite grasp the understanding of. I decided to take some more Shamanic training in London and on the weekend of the course, I had yet another powerful journey. I have had some influential journeys in my time and many experiences with Power Animals. I would like to

53

share this one in particular with you, which is very personal to me and so meaningful. It brought to me an understanding of who I am and about my life purpose.

I was taken to the lower world where my snowy owl waited to greet me. She took me with her as we flew to the middle world. I saw a vast lake encrusted with shimmering white ice. I looked down at my reflection, staring curiously back at myself from the chilled mirror effect. I tried to break through the crisp ice so that I could enter the lake. Beneath the water I saw two polar bears. They started to claw at the ice, and very quickly, a passage was made for me. I lowered myself slowly into the freezing water, holding my breath as I entered, waiting for the biting cold to overwhelm me and yet it was surprisingly comfortable.

I was completely naked and felt totally free—I was ecstatic. I felt weightless as I danced with the great ocean and swam with the two polar bears. I made it to the land where a pack of Arctic wolves waited for me. They were strikingly handsome with their white, winter coats. They stood there, so pristine, they had a bond so strong that nothing would ever come between them. I could sense the loyalty of the pack and I was overwhelmed with emotion, because I felt I belonged with them—that I was one of them. A moment later, I shape shifted into a strong female Arctic wolf and I walked towards my pack. They drew closer, in acknowledgement of me and then we playfully wrestled in the snow and nibbled at each other's ears. A feeling of tranquility came over me as I watched fluffy snowflakes falling from the sky across the full moon, hanging high above us. I beamed as I looked up towards the heavens and received blessings from the moon.

I looked around me, but no one else was there—all the other wolves were gone and I was on my own. I walked through the fresh snow for miles and miles until it gradually disappeared and spring had come.

There were gorgeous flowers everywhere and I especially

noticed groups of tall sunflowers, rising from the ground, supporting each other, as they swayed in the warm breeze. My body had now returned to my own naked form—I was no longer the wolf.

I stopped for a while to watch and admire the captivating scene ahead of me. I was so still and utterly quiet and then, out of nowhere, a swarm of bees landed all over me covering my entire body. Strangely, I was not afraid, but instead, I felt elated. The bees vanished, just as quickly as they had arrived. I checked my skin for any damage; I was amazed to find my whole body covered in soft golden honey. The bees had left their sweet syrup all over me.

I looked up to see a flock of brilliantly colored birds heading towards me. They landed on my body and began feeding on the honey. This started to tickle and made me giggle like a child. In a wonderful way, I felt as if I was helping these birds, nurturing them with the sugary nectar. Then, all at once, they too disappeared and I was immediately met by a rainbow colored butterfly. She came to take me with her—to fly into the rainbow that was arched across the sapphire sky.

We were flying freely together and when we reached the rainbow, we climbed up one side and slid down the other. I felt like a kid in a playground, until the gentle butterfly flew casually away and the rainbow faded. I became aware that it was starting to get dark. Soft, warm rain silently fell down, cleansing me. Without warning, I heard loud and fierce thunder. I glanced quickly up to the sky and saw an electrifying flash of lightening. Exhilarated by the power of the current and knowing no fear, I danced along with the thunder and lightening.

A council of men joined me—there were five of them. Their faces were hidden in a mist. These enlightened males who came to greet me had their hands filled with rattles and instruments and their bodies covered in furs and skins. Two of the men came closer to me and, as I lay down on the earth, they started to paint my body with their hands. I could smell sage burning and the smoke surrounded me. They painted me black and white, representing the male and female balance. With respect, they placed a wolf skin over my head and body. As I continued to dance, I started to become a wolf once again, transforming more and more into my precious wolf with every sound of thunder and each flash of lightning. This experience was becoming more real to me as I continued to dance and dance. The men disappeared through the fog. I did not have any desire to stop dancing. Then a large black raven came to join me and also danced—making me feel even more connected to the energy of the wolf and to myself—I became more and more empowered.

The drum beat faster and I felt it pounding in my chest. It intensified until it was time to return to reality, I made my way out of the journey. Through this encounter, I began to see more clearly the depths of my true purpose.

Step Four to Finding Your Life Purpose ~ Empowerment

Now take a moment for introspection. Be silent, close your eyes and take a deep breath. Is there a particular animal with whom you have always felt a connection to? Take another deep breath and ask which animal is guiding you at this very moment? What do you see? What can you hear? Notice your feelings towards this particular animal and take one more deep breath as you connect with the essence of your new friend. Does your Power Animal have a message for you? If so, what would it be? Give thanks for the wonderful new connection that you have made with this animal. Invite your Power Animal into your life to help you to feel, and be, more empowered.

CHAPTER FIVE

Encounters with a Sorceress

We are all individual beings with a purpose to fulfill on this earth,
to expand.
Awesome lands...so vibrant...enter my soul.
Awaken me...lift my spirit to the Understanding...the laughter.
Show me how to truly dream with the stars...
as I did when I was a child.
Enter me into your web of wisdom.
I am ready now to gain the knowledge...to hear the truth.
By embracing the darkness...I shall see the Sun.
Let the vibrant colors of my soul shine.

The old sorceress waits for me in a cavern underneath the red earth. She has been patiently longing for me to become a woman.

Her ancient wisdom resounds in my mind: 'To really experience being a woman, you must allow Mother Nature to evolve within you...to know what it is to be a mother yourself...to create a new life within your womb. You are ready now my child...you are a woman, a mother...a bringer of knowledge. It is time for you to blossom.'

Her name is Kauala. She is centuries old. Her fluorescent white hair and her glowing eyes were the only lights emanating from the dark cave. The russet colored dress she wore over her delicate frame, merged into the billowing red mist, rendering her almost invisible. I could barely see her form, it was as if she was a shadow—I almost felt scared by her presence. She was holding something in her bony hands. She released it and the most beautiful butterfly appeared. Its tiny, gossamer wings were subtle shades of pink, purple and silver—it almost did not look real. Pink for unconditional love, purple for my ability to inspire others and heal myself, and silver for the gateway between the two worlds — the spirit world and the earth.

She then pointed to my hand and placed a mysterious object inside it. It was a pen that seemed to turn different colors in the warmth of my hand. It reminded me of a mood ring that changes color to indicate the emotions of the wearer.

'You are to write a book,' she said.

Her voice was warm but firm, in keeping with her powerful aura and the authority of her words. I could feel my hand begin to vibrate and as I looked down, my fingers merged together and my hand transformed into a snake. This experience was so very potent. I started to feel stillness come over me and I could sense more of her energy. Despite being old and frail, her life force was vibrant and strong, but at the same time, very peaceful. It resonated throughout my body and soul and I felt calm. I understood that Kauala was my friend. She came not to scare me, but to empower me, in order to set me on my path towards my destiny.

My journey was at an end and so was the long flight. I had come out of my altered state of consciousness just as the plane was starting to land — we were in Brisbane.

'Wow! I am finally in Australia.'

I felt extremely excited, as I had been looking forward to visiting this country with Andy and Keanu, for a long time. We had five weeks to discover this awe-inspiring land. Our first destination was breathtaking Hamilton Island.

We settled into our resort and had a lovely meal in a local restaurant overlooking the ocean. Keanu especially enjoyed the company of a happy little visitor at the dining table. A lost little possum had come to greet him. Keanu was only five and a half years old at that time and so he found the intriguing distraction most welcome. After dinner, we headed back to our room where Andy and Keanu went straight to bed. I decided to use the opportunity to undertake a journey before I joined them.

As I listened to the hypnotic rhythm of the drumbeat, I

endeavored to reach the depths of the lower world, when I felt myself taken to the milder ambience of the middle world instead. I arrived in a desolate wilderness, standing barefoot on the red earth. An Australian Aboriginal woman, named Lia, met me. She was wearing a yellow skirt and a white, flowery blouse. Her hair was gray with swirls of white and just a hint of black still remained. Her face was old and tired. She told me her name comes from the 'Lia' flower, unbeknown to me. She held her hand out toward me and welcomed me to her ancestral village.

Lia referred to me as 'dearest one.' She drew a circle in the earth with a sharp stick.

I intuitively knew that it was a symbol for the world and as she pointed to the center, she proclaimed, 'You are here and the world is all around you.' Her voice was commanding, but kind as she continued, 'You need to find your place on this earth...you need to find where in this circle you want to position yourself. You have not yet found your position in the world...there is a force, like the wind, blowing you in many different directions. You have been trying to control the wind...let it take you.'

She smiled at me with much warmth and I smiled back. I knew she was right.

'You are like a young bird getting frustrated, because you do not yet have the wings to fly. You have not allowed yourself to become free inside. Come now...come with me and I will show you something significant that will be of help to you.'

We walked together in the dry heat to a hillside next to a small stream. She put her hands into a jagged hole and pulled out a turquoise colored rock.

'If you close your eyes you can get inside this stone and dream...dream with it,' Lia said in a firm tone. 'Let it take you inside of yourself...that is where you will find your true purpose...your soul purpose. Stay with it a while and you will understand more, when you are ready to.'

After what seemed like an eternity, but was really only a few short minutes, I knew it was time to leave. I reached for the rock and held it tightly. Lia led me back to the spot where we had first met and when I turned around to walk away from her, a gate closed behind us and she silently disappeared. I looked down at my left hand and an exquisite yellow and white flower lay in my palm.

'Maybe this is a "Lia" flower,' I thought.

I gazed upward at the Universe and an immaculate star, bright in the midnight blue sky, shone its silvery light down upon me. I knew then that Lia was still with me and I felt a wonderful wave of serenity flow into my heart.

'I have made a very special friend,' I thought to myself, as I returned to reality, back in the hotel room.

Andy and Keanu were still sleeping and I felt happy knowing they were safe and well in their dreams. With Lia's voice still fresh in my mind, I settled myself down to sleep.

'Let your spirit sing...let your spirit sing,' her words drifted through my mind.

My feelings and thoughts were united in the belief that we are all here to let our spirit sing. We are creative individuals with many different talents. It is when we entwine these unique qualities together with our soul's purpose that we can truly shine.

I was almost asleep when I had a remarkably vivid vision. There was a dark mist swirling all around me.

I could hear a woman's voice—Lia was standing in the direction of the north, 'They said you would return again for us to dream together. You must cooperate. We cannot do this without your courage.'

A man stood in the direction of the west—he was painted in black. He was an Australian Aboriginal man with strong features and curly, shoulder-length hair. He looked very relieved to see me. His ebony eyes filled with tears as he stared at me.

'Time lines,' he said. 'You are now ready to receive what is necessary to take you further on the path of your dreams...you are the dream...you are already in it...free yourself,' he said with great conviction.

The man suddenly disappeared and I could hear the voice of Kauala, chanting a song. I could not quite make out the words, but I knew it was something special. Her image was becoming more visible now, as the fog was dissolving. In the distance I could see a friendly face with a warming smile.

She stopped singing and she began to speak to me, 'I'm so happy to see you. I have waited one hundred years to meet with you again...that is when you were last here, for your initiation. You have carried much pain since you were a young girl. Let yourself be free, my child. Transform now...you no longer need to bear the burden. You carry your birthright...you are ready to be an individual and create what you are meant to become...there is a time in life for all things. You must choose to stay where you are, safe in your cave, or allow your fears to fade and truly live...choose well, for when your worries have vanished...only then can you soar.'

After that, her voice seemed distant. I remember that I felt warm and then I was asleep.

If you choose to acknowledge your pain, only when you really understand it, can you let it go. It has served its purpose. You will then have the opportunity to evolve into something magnificent. There are always choices in life; I believe that we create our own future through our choices. There comes a time when you need to ask yourself: Is it worth hanging on to or is it time to choose to move on?

The next morning, Keanu woke us up bright and early. I could see the sun rising majestically over the water. Andy had planned to go on a fishing trip, while I spent the day snorkeling at the Great Barrier Reef. I was so thrilled — the last time I had snorkeled was many years earlier in the Bahamas. Keanu was looking forward to spending the day playing in the kids club.

When I got back from my outing, I decided to sit on the pure white sand for a while before picking Keanu up from playgroup. I sat there and thought about my vision and the journeys I experienced the night before.

I noticed a man who was sitting on the beach reading a book. He had long white hair and looked very wise—almost wizard-like. He wore reading glasses on the edge of his nose and a canvas hat with a buzzard feather hanging from it, shaded him from the warm afternoon sun. His appearance gave him a look of being well-traveled. He seemed to be in his seventies, but he was glowing with a youthful essence.

'Why am I so interested in this man?' I thought to myself.

As I stared at him, I imagined him changing into a radiant youth and then back into himself again. I reflected on the many different faces we carry.

We are all perfectly unique individuals, all on our life's journey, going in many different directions. What weaves us together is that we are all trying to live our lives the best way we can. How many past lives have we come through? Are we trying to correct mistakes that we made in a former existence?

I started to think more about my spirituality and the many places in the world that I have connected with, wondering if I had been in Australia before, in a previous lifetime. Maybe Lia and the old sorceress were right—I am on this earth to fulfill my mission, just as we all are, but what if we have not quite understood what we are supposed to have learned? What if we have spent many lifetimes and still not found our purpose? Surely, there is a way of knowing if that is true. We sometimes meet people or connect to the energy of certain places as a way of continuing our journey of life.

I looked down at my feet in the sand and dug them deeper into the earth.

'This is why we are all here,' I thought. 'To find peace, balance and harmony within one another's footsteps.' My thoughts became enlightened, 'We must, however, start with ourselves, by going deep within and really finding out what makes us who we are? What drives us? What inspires us to live? Are we ruled by our heads instead of our hearts?'

It was time for me to collect Keanu and Andy's fishing charter boat was due in. Our time on this spectacular Island was ending tomorrow and we would continue our journey to other parts of Australia.

We arrived at Ayers Rock (or Uluru as the aboriginal people call it). What a bewitching place this was. We had heard that the rock changes color to reflect its mood and we were looking forward to seeing this anomaly. As we began to walk around Uluru we could not believe the amount of flies everywhere. We were told that, for some reason, this year, there was an unusual abundance of them. The flies were becoming a nuisance, going in our mouths and up our noses, so Keanu and I purchased face nets to cover our heads. However, they still found a way of smothering our faces and, at one point, Andy must have had a thousand flies on his back. We began hitting him to get them off, much to his annoyance. Nevertheless, we all enjoyed the spectacular scenery.

After dinner we went straight back to our room, as I was eager to take a Shamanic journey before I fell asleep. I wanted to see if I could connect with the old lady in the cave once more.

The beat from my drumming CD led me to the red earth and then to the cave where a large, green python lay blocking the entrance. I reached out my hand towards the serpent, as I knew he wanted me to hold him. As I picked up the python, he began to wriggle and writhe. I felt that the sinewy snake was challenging me and testing my endurance. Then he relaxed and I felt more at ease. He started guiding me to the old sorceress. There she was, waiting for me.

'Come child... come closer and walk with me.'

She extended her hand for me to follow her.

'Understand what the spirit is... We all have one. The mystery unfolds, you know... You will find yours through your words.'

Kauala and I continued to wander through the cave until we reached a water hole.

'Come and sit here,' she said. 'Life is a gift... you just need to understand it. Know the corners of the world, so that when the strong wind calls, you will hear it, when the moonlit sky glows, you will see it and when the refreshing raindrops fall, you will feel them cleanse you.'

She picked up a piece of black tourmaline and she held it before me. Like a magnet, the powerful stone drew out all of the impurities and negativity from my body. She then took rose quartz and amethyst crystals and put them in front of my body. I felt as though they were integrating into my being. I looked at her in disbelief as she suddenly transformed into a youthful woman with blonde hair and blue eyes.

'Who are you?' I asked.

'It is I,' she replied. 'We must all leave our good prints on the sand so that children of future generations may follow into our footsteps...we are all here to share with one another. This is balance...when power is manipulated it will diminish like dust in the wind. You come here for wisdom...I give you creativity.'

She showed me the colors orange and blue in the form of a cloth, which she wrapped around me and then, stepping back, she smiled. She took out an herb and white smoke started to fill the cave. I could sense she was about to perform some kind of ritual or healing. Kauala reached over to touch my navel and began pulling a substance out of it. I could feel the pressure as it was leaving my body. I didn't want to look as I was petrified, but out of curiosity I glanced down to see the ancient woman extract something dark and grotesque and it was no longer inside of me.

'Guilt!' She exclaimed. 'That was releasing the guilt that you have carried for many years and you are now ready to receive more wisdom for your journey.'

She replaced it by putting energy, in the form of a bright light, back into my navel.

She continued to teach me. 'We all make choices in our lives...you must not feel guilty for those choices. Why do you opt to bring stress into your life? You people become so busy with your lifestyles...it is too easy to forget the spirit. Every now and again you need to detach from this and allow your spirit to wander...well it never really wanders...for the soul always knows where it is going.'

The young woman then transformed back into the sorceress and escorted me to the entrance of the cave. It was time to leave, as I could hear the call back of the drum. I knew that I could return and visit her anytime I needed to, as she would always be there for me. I felt honored and gave thanks to her. As I began to reflect on what I had just experienced, I was reminded of when I held my very first snake on a trip to Thailand. For many years, I was afraid of snakes but an opportunity presented itself in Bangkok to, at last, overcome my phobia. I placed a python around my neck, an act in which I empowered myself by facing a deep-seated dread. We have all known some form of trepidation and I think it is very healthy to face these fears. Sometimes our phobias can be so great that they prevent us from moving forward, or becoming more successful.

The next morning, we were excited to go back to see Uluru. We wondered if the color of the rock would look different today. It started raining and we had read somewhere that if it rains whilst you are at Ayers Rock, it means that one day you will return. We arrived just in time to witness an eye-catching sight, as jagged streaks of white lightning pierced the sky over the rock. It was mesmerizing. I felt so very blessed for our family to have seen this and I knew that we would visit here again.

Step Five to Finding your Life Purpose ~ Expand

Now take a moment for introspection. Be silent, close your eyes and take a deep breath. Ask yourself, what is your life purpose? Now ask yourself, what would you like it to be? Are both answers the same? If not, don't you think they should be? Why are you here? How does your presence affect others? Can you remember back to when you were a child, what did you want to be when you grew up? What inspires you? Breathe it all in and feel the love and light spread through your entire body. Take another deep breath and go deep down into your very core—where the truth resides. Now ask that you fully awaken to understanding your life purpose. Are you ready to hear the answer? Are you ready to expand?

CHAPTER SIX

Understanding Your Roots ~ Healing Your Past to Step into Your Future

Breathe in the air, that of your ancestors.
Place your feet on the earth, this is your domain.
You have finally found it, your home.
The mystery is revealed, you know where you are going, at last.
Love, affection, culture, is yours.

It was eleven pm and I could feel my temperature starting to rise. I had been violently ill for hours. I had not been this sick since my trip to Fiji, but at least this time I was at home. One month had gone by since we got back from Australia and after all the traveling we had done, I was glad to be back in familiar surroundings. I recognized the nausea as my body's way of ridding itself of the emotional debris that I was still hanging on to. I could hardly stand up, because I was so weak and my legs had turned to jelly. I crawled into bed and immediately fell into a deep sleep, only to wake up a few hours later in a tepid pool of my own sweat.

I was burning up with a high fever and my nightdress was soaking wet. I started to hallucinate and for a moment, I saw a Mediterranean woman standing next to our bed, playing the tambourine. She looked familiar to me and then I realized it was the same lady I had seen in a journey the previous day. She looked Italian or ancient Greek and she wore gypsy-like clothing, which was reminiscent of a belly dancing costume. The exotic outfit was made of a sheer fabric— turquoise in color. It was intriguing, because I've always been interested in belly dancing, but I had only recently signed up for classes. The woman was of medium build. She had dark brown, shoulder-length hair and she smiled repeatedly, but would never show her teeth (I wondered if she had any at all).

In my journey, she had taken me to the upper world, where I saw a beautiful bright shining star, twinkling in the twilit sky. It looked to be made of gleaming gold, with inner sparkles emanating from its diamond encrusted core. I was admiring the scintillating star when it serendipitously appeared in my hands. I gazed at it in awe. The more I stared, the more it shone, until it was glowing so intensely, I had to avert my eyes. Beaming brilliantly, the dazzling star became alive, dancing in circles around me.

The scene swiftly changed to that of a hospital room. It was as if I was watching a movie on a big screen. I saw myself as a tiny baby, after my mother had just given birth to me and I heard my first cry into this new world. I saw an image of a man moving towards me—he was a Native American. I stared at him, as he drew closer, studying every line on his distinguished face. Amazingly, he turned into a wise old wizard, with a long white beard and a stream of silvery hair cascading down his back. His discerning eyes looked directly into mine and then, to my dismay, he started to fade. An image of another man appeared—it was my father. He stood in front of me with a vacant expression on his face and then he also disappeared. Eventually, the Native American man reappeared. He was very old with long, gray hair. He spoke slowly, in a very soft voice.

'Time will tell,' he said.

I had taken this Shamanic journey to help me understand my roots. I wanted to learn more about the history of my father's side of the family. I did not know much about my dad's heritage, because my parents had moved to Toronto from Calabria many years before I was born and they divorced when I was around one year old. I have never really known my father, as he has been hospitalized ever since I was a small girl.

I had not been to Italy for about fifteen years. The last time I went was with my sister, when I was twenty. We took a trip to Europe and we spent a lot of our time in Calabria with our mother's relatives. It was a joyful trip that we will never forget. We visited with our uncle (a well-known doctor in the village), our aunt and our cousins. However, we did not connect with any of our father's relations. I felt that, in some way, I could not move forward until I fully understood why I had been born into this family, in this lifetime and what it was that I had to learn from it all.

It was now three o'clock in the morning. I woke my husband.

'I need to go back to Italy,' I said, unceremoniously in the darkness. 'We need to go to Italy,' I repeated. 'I need to connect with my roots and find out all about my ancestors.'

Andy was half asleep and told me we would discuss it in the morning, but I had such a strong feeling about this, that I could not let it go. I no longer felt sick, only drained from the experience.

We are all descendants from a long lineage of different ancestors and it is my belief that we cannot truly know ourselves until we fully understand the seed from which we have grown. Where is our place of origin? Who are our parents? Why were we born into our family? Some say that we select our own parents and if that is true, then why did we choose them? No matter what our situation, we have been brought into this world for a purpose—a reason to live—to simply be. When we have unlocked the mysteries within us, we can be healed of ignorance. Our relationship with our parents may have been a happy one, a sad one, or even a painful one, but once we have deeply connected with and understood our situation, then we are healed, forgiven and we can build stronger relationships with our family and others.

We can begin by feeling gratitude and giving thanks to our parents for bringing us into this world. We can give blessings and celebrate them for listening to our call, our choice to have been born at that time. We are on a sacred mission—our life is a divine journey. What have we learned from being born into this family? What special gifts have we gained that were passed down from generation to generation? If we could change something, what would it be and why? Is there anything that needs to be forgiven or celebrated, which is directly related to our parents or ancestors?

I had all these questions going through my mind, over and over again. I had been lying awake for hours. It was morning now and my fever had finally broken. I decided it was time for me to search further into my past, because I knew that it would bring about a healing for me. I needed to forgive the past before it destroyed my happiness. I was also at a point in my life where I was finally ready to know the truth. I told Andy again how I desperately desired to connect with my roots, but he didn't need much persuading, because he likes to travel just as much as I do. We booked our trip to Southern Italy for the end of December.

The moment we arrived in Naples I tried brushing up on my Italian. I got by, but I hoped that they would understand my dialect better in Calabria. We picked up our hire-car near to the airport, what a job that was...and then we began the long journey to the hotel. Thank goodness I wasn't doing any of the driving, because when it comes to lane discipline and road etiquette, the drivers that we encountered left something to be desired! It seemed like they all had to be somewhere in such a hurry, as if their lives depended on it. Fortunately, Andy is more experienced behind the wheel than I am and so we arrived at our destination safe and sound, if not a little shaken.

We checked into our seafront hotel in the village where my mother was born. It is a picturesque little village, nestled against the alluring Ionian Sea. It was made even more attractive by the Christmas lights, which were still up and by a beautiful nativity display, which adorned the square in front of the church. We would be here to see in the new year and I explained to Keanu all about the Bafana (the kind old witch who came to visit the children, that had been good, in the first week of January and filled their stockings with treats). That evening we went to visit my aunt, a warm, loving woman, who always filled a room with cheer and smiles and we enjoyed some of her delicious pasta, in the company of my cousins.

The next day, the weather was balmy, a lot warmer than it was in England at that time of year. I went to see my cousins from my father's side of the family, whom I hadn't met before. By speaking to them I was able to trace back to some other relatives that I never even knew about. One of them was my cousin, Antonio, who offered to be our guide.

He took us to see some of the fabulous sights and scenery in the area, like the quaint old town of Gerace and the charming island of Sicily. Antonio is a very humorous and expressive man, who loves to talk. He seemed fascinated by Andy and would go on and on at him in Italian. Poor Andy couldn't understand a word of what he was saying to him. I tried explaining this to Antonio, but he didn't seem to mind and carried on regardless.

I wanted to visit the graveyard where my grandmother was buried. It is up in the mountains, but we did not know exactly where. Antonio said he knew where it was, so he agreed to take us there. We must have taken a wrong turn somewhere and we had to ask for directions. We stopped to speak to a mountain man, who was unshaven and wore scruffy clothes, but seemed very friendly. He was about to tell us how to get to the cemetery when his wife interrupted him. His features suddenly became contorted with rage and his eyes looked like they were about to pop out of his head. He said something extremely derogatory to his wife in Italian and, at this point, we noticed he was brandishing a shotgun. Antonio's expression turned to one of shock and panic. He made our excuses and we couldn't get out of there fast enough. If it wasn't for the seriousness of it, the situation would have been quite comical.

71

We never did find the graveyard, but many of my father's relatives live up in the mountains, so I met more of my cousins and learned everything I could about my heritage. This was a very healing time for me, because I had always closed myself off to anything related to my father and I had never known much about him or his background. By the end of the holiday many of the questions that I had were finally answered and I was able to have some kind of closure on them. I felt much more at peace with everything that had troubled me and I was not as clueless as before. It was an added bonus having my family with me. Andy had a great time, despite the language barrier, particularly enjoying the Italian culture and hospitality and Keanu had a surprise visit from the Bafana, who brought him lots of amazing Christmas goodies.

After retuning home from Italy, I was still processing and digesting everything that had happened to me on the trip. In order to reflect further, I sat quietly and meditated for a while. I became so relaxed in my meditation that I started to go into an unplanned soul journey. I found myself somewhere in the mountains of Montana.

I could hear a voice drifting out of the distance, 'Fatherless child…a void inside of you awaits to be filled with love…love that only a father can give…you are loved and will always be loved.'

It was a man's voice and, as he began to move closer towards me, I realized it was the Native American man I had seen in a previous journey, after my mother had just given birth to me.

I spoke to him and called him father, 'Since I was a little girl, I have always wondered where you were and I have longed for this moment to be fully with you.'

My heart began to feel heavy as I continued, 'It is only now I am a grown woman that you stand before me.'

There was a lump in my throat and I had to choke back the tears.

'Why have I found you now?' I asked him.

'Now is not the end for us…just the beginning…this bond will never die…the union of father and daughter can never be erased,' he stated emphatically.

He came closer still and embraced me with his warm and sincere presence of unconditional love—the longing that I had as a child, to be held and loved so dearly by my father, had been fulfilled. I held him tightly with so much affection.

His fragile, aged body began to collapse. I supported his weight and we made our way up the side of a luscious green mountain.

All the while I reassured him by saying, 'I have you father and will never let you go…not ever.'

He looked at me with total conviction. It took all of the strength I could muster, but we eventually reached the summit. Just at that very moment he became lighter. I watched him as he slowly faded into my arms and then, like dust in the wind, he was gone. My heart was about to burst, as the pain and anguish that had been buried deep inside of me started to surface. My emotions finally escaped the prison of my body and flooded out of me like a fierce, flowing waterfall. My grief overwhelmed me, my aqueous tears transforming into an acceptance, somewhere within my being—I had finally recognized and honored my father for who he is, rather than for what he had done, or the mistakes he might have made. His soul entered into this world for its own particular purpose. This purpose was one that some people may never agree with, as his journey has been a sad one. It was time for me to let go of the burden that had haunted me for most of my life. For the first time ever…I was free. I had never known him, but I saw that his essence had taught me many things. I finally knew what it was like to feel absolute autonomy.

I looked up to the sky and the most majestic eagle was soaring overhead. He circled high above me seven times and then took off, flying until he was just a mere spec on the horizon. I saw something falling from the heavens. I cupped my hands together and hoped to catch this wonderful offering from above. There it was, it fell straight into my anticipating hands—the eagle had gifted me a plume.

From the echoes of the eagle's cry, I heard a voice, 'Your spirit is so strong...I knew you would find me.'

That is the last thing I heard before I came out of my trance. As soon as I was fully conscious again, I instinctively grabbed for my pen and paper and wrote this:

A stranger to me...but familiar to my soul. Spread your great wings of deliverance. Soar like the eagle does...for the gates of Heaven await you. Fly father...fly to freedom at last!

The trip to Italy, which had taken me back to my parent's hometown, was extremely therapeutic for me. I regained a part of myself that had been deeply abandoned—lost in immense confusion. I am so very humble and grateful for this incredible path that I walk.

I no longer search for the past, as I have left that far behind me. I have gained a new knowledge and I grasp my future with belief in myself, as I embrace my culture. I honor and respect my parents—who they are and where they came from.

There is a key to inner knowledge that each of us holds and only we know, deep down inside of our core, what our own truth may be. Sometimes, it can take a little more soul searching than we might have anticipated. We should be kind to ourselves when we embark on the inner journey. We may encounter fragile and unknown territories, so we must tread with care and know that there will always be illumination to escort us to the place where we need to be. As our trail unfolds, step by step, the mysteries deep within will also unravel, as we continue to travel our life's journey.

Step Six to Finding Your Life Purpose ~ Essence

Now take a moment for introspection. Be silent, close your eyes and take a deep breath. Connect with the essence of your mother. What have you learned from one another in this lifetime? Now connect with the essence of your father. What have your learned from each other in this lifetime? Why do you think you were born into this family? Take another deep breath and as you inhale, honor your parents and give thanks to them, also honor yourself and your heritage.

CHAPTER SEVEN

The Inward Journey to Healing ~ Soul Retrieval

You are free, whole as can be.
There is true freedom within you.
Feel the soft breeze blowing gently on your face.
When the wind of chaos calls, it will pass you by.
For now you stand tall, tall as a tree, and not a leaf will fall.

'Lia, where are you?' I asked.

'I am still here child,' she whispered softly. 'Sometimes you may not see or hear me...but you are getting closer to finding out who you really are. You are near to your truth...life is becoming interesting, isn't it?'

Her voice still lingered in my mind as she murmured, 'You did it...you moved out of the center of the circle. You are getting closer to your destination.'

'What destination?' I asked, wanting to know more.

Her reply was intriguing, 'You will see...it is good...you are on the road to adventure again...back in the great mystery where you belong. This is where you thrive...where you go to unravel the meaning of the knowledge you have been given—your hidden truths, child. There is much ahead of you...many synchronicities will follow. Remember to obey your heart...you will be guided. Your heart is strong...do not question it. The mysteries are waiting to be revealed.'

She spoke with such certainty.

'I don't understand,' I exclaimed, feeling a little weary.

'You do not need to understand right now...' she replied. 'Just follow your heart. This is good...you are ready...you are passing through the shadows. When the blackness comes it is only an opening...see it as thus...go through the passageway and surrender. Do not fight it...for this is the darkness we sometimes need to experience...to find our spark again.'

She continued in a reassuring tone, 'You have searched your soul long enough for the knowledge of your past. Now it is time to search for the knowledge of your future. The world is shifting... many changes are coming. The earth has waited a very long time for these changes... they are close. You will remain on the earth to witness and be a part of this odyssey. Be ready...be prepared...hold on firmly because the ride is near. You will not wish to get off...you will not want the euphoria to end...but understand this, child...everyone must come off at some time...life is not possible without the balancing of the two realms—my world of the spirit and your earthly one. That is what keeps the scales of your being in equilibrium...there must be harmony between both worlds. Another chapter is beginning for you...seek and you shall find...your truth is approaching.'

'What truth?' I asked.

'You will understand soon...' she replied in her mysterious way. 'But for now go to sleep...I shall be with you in the dreamtime.'

Why is it that we all tend to stay in the place within ourselves that we have grown accustomed to and are comfortable in? Why are we so frightened to move on? Why do we feel the need to hang on to something? It was time to release all of my excess baggage. I had already let go of so much, yet still there was more. I had to find out what I was hanging on to that I no longer required. Was it anger, fear, guilt or maybe shame? Whatever it was had taunted me long enough. I knew that it was no good for me and that it had caused me pain. I wanted to allow the unfamiliar to enter my world, to welcome fresh possibilities into my life and permit new doors to open. I first needed to 'empty my suitcase,' remove the negative so that I could then refill it with the positive, to prepare for future voyages—the next phase in my life. There were golden opportunities awaiting.

I recognized there were specific things that happened in my life that I needed to take a deeper look into. I was experiencing the feeling that something was not quite right with my emotions. Thankfully, my spiritual path was growing stronger, so I contacted a Shamanic practitioner to see if I had any 'soul loss.'

Many people have asked me about the expression 'soul loss.' They wonder if it is really possible to loose a part of one's soul. It is a term used in Shamanism when people become disconnected from a part of themselves and they do not quite feel whole, leaving a feeling of disempowerment. They may feel cut off from a part of their psyche and in some cases, are not in complete control of their thoughts, feelings or actions. The soul has fragmented and needs to be repaired, made whole again, as described in Sandra Ingerman's book, *Soul Retrieval, Mending The Fragmented Self*. Most of us have experienced some kind of trauma in our life, whether it be from an accident, illness, loss, shock, break up of a relationship, or some form of abuse. The experience may have been too overwhelming and difficult to deal with at the time and therefore, a part of us—the damaged and weakened part of our psyche, simply leaves us, so we can continue with our lives. When this happens it might leave us feeling empty, like there is a huge void inside.

Some people who have experienced 'soul loss' have said they feel spaced-out and have trouble focusing. Others say they feel lifeless and powerless and they have not been the same since the incident. It can also bring on depression, feelings of anger and irritability or heightened emotions, not normally associated with their own character. When somebody suffering from 'soul loss' is ready to receive healing, a suitably trained Shamanic practitioner can perform a soul retrieval for them. Through the guidance of their spirit helpers, the practitioner will take a journey to first locate the missing soul part, where upon it is then returned to the person, allowing them to feel complete and whole again. This journey is not to be taken lightly, as it is often very serious and deep work. It is important to be properly prepared and to brace oneself for such a perilous journey.

Throughout my spiritual journey I have dealt with my own 'soul loss.' One of my most life altering occurrences was during my training as a Shamanic practitioner, in a workshop for soul retrieval. I was partnered up with a stranger to perform soul retrievals for each other. Our teacher had chosen us to work together, not knowing anything about either of us and had no idea that our circumstances were very similar—in fact, there was such a strong connection between us that we subsequently became good friends.

I believe there are no coincidences in life. We meet people and are put into situations, because there is a higher intention which, at that time, is beyond our comprehension. These situations, for me, have always been validated. It turned out we both shared similar traumatic experiences in our lives when we were children (in my case being sexually abused on various occasions) and we had both been left feeling more broken and in pieces than we had ever imagined possible. I was aware of the sense of loss on a deep level, but I did not want to acknowledge it and I did not know the effect that it had on my life, until it came forward dramatically, during my own soul retrieval.

My partner had successfully reunited me with my missing soul part. Now it was my turn. This was the darkest journey that I had undertaken, to date—to restore power for her and at the same time, to keep my own soul intact.

During my journey, I was taken to a dark, dank tunnel that had a musty smell to it. It led me to an eerie underworld—a place where absent souls existed. A skeleton guide was waiting there for me. He took me to the cave of lost children, where I was able to retrieve the missing soul part for her. I brought it back safely, enabling her to welcome a part of her essence back that had been gone for so long.

After the workshop, I took a journey to meet with the lost part of me that had been so fragmented. This was a very beautiful journey for me.

I arrived at a peaceful old willow tree, where I found the little girl Rosanna (myself as a child) sitting under it in blissful contentment. She was wearing a pretty pink dress and her aura was simply gleaming.

She smiled at me radiantly and whispered, 'You must learn to be more gentle and to love yourself.'

(I had not been able to love myself, because like many of us, I had some attributes that I did not like, let alone love.) I joined her under the tree.

'It is important to fully embrace all that you are, if you want to become whole again,' she said.

Then I saw my first dog, Snoopy, approaching. He was part Cocker Spaniel with a scruffy, black and white coat. He had been in my life since I was one year old, until the age of eighteen. I absolutely adored him. Snoopy came and sat down beside us. We were all now sheltered under a cozy canopy of protection, as we absorbed the healing energy emanating from the elegant tree. As a feeling of assurance washed over me, I was shown the incident where the soul loss happened. In that instant, most of the insecurities that I had in my life disappeared and the dark feeling that I sensed for so long, lifted and was replaced with a happy one. I was empowered and over flowing with confidence. I knew that I could succeed at anything I set my mind to. I was honoring myself for bravely overcoming my fear.

We embraced one another and ambled towards a stunning, scarlet and saffron sunset. As we drew closer the fiery glow of the setting sun spread out across the sky and in the distance, I saw a rattlesnake and a tarantula coming to greet us. The snake was authoritative, but this did not intimidate me, because I could feel his shielding energy—as if he was my bodyguard. The spider was dark and furry and she had a soft, almost shy, appearance.

However, this was not to be mistaken for weakness. They were my protectors, my new Power Animals, who had come to assist me with the healing. I breathed in this spectacular scene and on my third gasp, the little girl Rosanna had integrated fully into my being. I took another deep breath and I could feel the oneness—I was whole again.

I transformed into a great golden eagle, merging into the awe-inspiring sunset, expanding my vast wings of freedom to join the sun and all of life. The Eagle perched on the peak of a majestic mountain and suddenly turned into a graceful goddess. She had the poise of a swan, her long flowing hair, swaying softly in the gentle breeze. She was emblazoned in sumptuous silk robes, in delicate shades of purple, pink and turquoise. My essence entwined with her elegance, beauty and strength—she was I...I was she...with that knowledge I felt victorious.

A powerful elk came to meet me. I mounted his muscular back and held on to his enormous antlers with all of my might. We strolled through the forest that was filled with colorful autumn leaves, covering the earth with their beauty, and passed awesome oak trees that adorned an ancient forest. I felt like I had new eyes and was seeing everything in a different light.

As we arrived at a clearing, we were bathed in silvery moonbeams. The dewy meadow glistened in the silky moonlight. I jumped off the elk and began to howl at the moon. The elk vanished and I shape-shifted into the form of a female timber wolf. A male wolf came to greet me and we both started to walk up a grass-covered hill. We rubbed noses and howled together through this glorious green glade. When we both finished howling, we could hear the echoes of our souls awakening the woodland. The male wolf disappeared and I turned back into myself again.

I walked back to my willow tree and danced around it joyously. I danced many times and then on the seventh, I was joined by four green and orange hummingbirds and three prismatic butterflies. It was as if I was a child again, only this time playing freely with no burdens or worries.

My soul retrieval had given me the opportunity to become fully present within myself. After that journey, I welcomed back my soul part and I felt that, not only had the missing piece of me returned, but that it was sealed inside of me forever.

Six years later, I had different issues going on in my life, but I was experiencing the same symptoms that I recognized as 'soul loss.' I went to see the Shamanic practitioner I had contacted and during a journey she took on my behalf, her teachers told her that I was not quite ready to have soul retrieval, but she was guided to 'rattle' over me. Rattles are powerful tools used in Shamanism. The shaking of the rattle can be used to stimulate the higher frequency passageway in the brain. Many cultures use both the drum and rattle. In my experience, the rattle is used to call upon the spirit helpers, healing the body by unlocking blockages that have been stored in different parts and also to assist with extractions. There are many kinds of rattles and some cultures have very beautifully decorated ones, my favorite being of the Southwestern region of the United States.

Whilst she did this, I was aware of the healing energy emanating from the rattle and from the teachers that were assisting her. I could feel a shift happening within my body.

After the session, I thanked her and was grateful for the assistance. Less than an hour later, I was amazed that a memory resurfaced. It was becoming clearer and clearer in my mind. I had a sudden awakening about an incident involving a friend, which I had buried inside of me for many years. This so-called friend had taken advantage of me, imposing his energy without my permission. What is inside someone that makes them think they have the right to invade another's sacred body temple? I remember in that desperate moment that I escaped somewhere in my mind, trying to convince myself that it was okay. I had become accustomed to patterns of abuse and it continued until I had the courage to stop being the victim and I owned up to the truth. The truth is that we push things aside, thinking that they can be forgotten and buried... until they chew and chew at us, consuming a huge chunk of our being and taking over our lives. I believe that deeply rooted issues will eventually arise in one form or another—like open wounds that never heal, because they have not been given the special attention it requires for the healing to take place. However, the soul knows when we are ready to face them. When this happens, we must be brave and confront the situation with great courage.

When we stop running from the reality and start forgiving, then we can move forward with pure strength and dignity, allowing wonderful things to enter our lives. I became very upset and told my husband all about the event that had caused me so much distress and had left me feeling so powerless. I had never told anyone about the incident before. I suppressed it to the back of my mind, thinking it would never come to light.

I knew that as I was on the road to recovery—there were no more secrets. Everything had to surface if I truly wanted to be in complete harmony with myself. It had been submerged in me for a very long time, but I was now, on some level, ready to deal with the issue. I was astounded how this Shamanic practitioner, with only the power of the rattle and the guidance of her helpers, had managed to unlock the pain inside of me that was causing this 'soul loss.' In order for me to continue on my path as a teacher and a healer, I knew that it was vital for me to undergo a soul retrieval. I eventually underwent the soul retrieval on a different occasion— when I was ready for it, enabling me to completely release the burden that I had endured for so long. If there is a situation in your life that you need to resolve, how you achieve the change is not important—what matters, is that you set yourself free.

I could see Lia in my mind's eye.

'Hear my voice, child...it is on the wind and in the raindrops that gently fall in the forest. Your heart is blooming and ready to show your inspiration. It is time for you to expand…you are so much more than you know. Like lightening cracking open a walnut…your core is unveiled and your uniqueness is ready to explode. Your imagination is beyond belief…take my hand and come join the celebration of your pilgrimage—your life's mission.'

I walked with Lia as she took me to a celestial place, where I was blinded by a brilliant array of colors. It was as if I was walking through them one by one, deep purple, electric blue, luminescent pink…they were so full of life. The amazing colors danced all over my body and were absorbed into my being. My hands twirled effortlessly in the rays and hues of the rainbow colors, making movements that I have never done before. It was as if I was involved in some sacred feminine ritual. I moved into the celebration until I became the celebration—bringing and blending all the vibrant colors of the world together. I could sense the deep, divine feminine within myself and I felt like a true Goddess.

Lia had a different look on her face, one that I had not seen before—she stood proudly, like a mother watching her child performing a newly acquired skill. This was no performance, this was my sacred dance—my dance of life. I had spent so many years in darkness, healing from my wounds and searching deep within for understanding and wisdom. I was now finally basking in the sunlight—the light that I had been so reluctant to find. I was ready to embark on a whole new voyage, but what would I do with all the brightness that I now carried? Was I afraid of seeing how much luminosity I really had within me? Why are we often apprehensive about expanding and shining our brightest beacons? We are so much more than we think we are; isn't it time that you unveiled your greatest mystery?

The time had come to go even deeper into a different realm altogether…the kingdom where pure light resides—where my greatest gifts were laying waiting for me. This expedition of illumination was not an easy one, but once I had embraced it, with intention and purity of purpose, it turned out to be the most rewarding voyage I had taken so far.

I could hear Lia's voice once more, 'Great transformation of awaited desire. The time is now...the star has fallen. It fell from the sky and into your hands of conception. You have seen the vision...now create it, live it and be it...with your greatest beauty. Shine, child...shine the brightest light that you have ever known.'

Step Seven to Finding Your Life Purpose ~ Forgiveness

Now take a moment for introspection. Be silent, close your eyes and take a deep breath.

Allow the wind of your soul to speak to you. Is there anything in your life that you have buried deep inside and would like to examine? Take another deep breath and now connect with your inner child. What does this child look like? What messages about yourself would you like to know? Is there a person or situation in your life that you feel needs to be forgiven? Take another deep breath and as you exhale, gently release what you want to let go of. Ask that you may have the strength and compassion to forgive.

CHAPTER EIGHT

Angels, Fairies, Saints and Healing with Crystals

Inspiration, Aspiration, Imagination, Manifestation.
Reaching your heights with no limitations.
Create your desires and dream.
Take me there, where I want to be.
Visions take me to eternity.

Angels

Do you ever wonder if you have Angels watching over you? I have believed in the angelic realm, since I was a little girl—an Angel would often wake me in the middle of the night. I remember one time, being given a beautiful, deep red spirit-rose. These graceful hands were reaching over me and they gently placed the delicate flower into my grasp. As I accepted this gift, the healing energy coming from it was radiating into my hands. On a different occasion, I sensed that there were Angels surrounding my bed. When I looked up, fresh, cleansing snowflakes were falling softly on my face.

Another instance was a surprise visit from a serene little cherub. She came to visit me in the early hours (it was around two am). I opened my eyes and saw a mist surrounding this adorable little girl—her face was innocent and pure. The experience was so surreal, I thought that maybe I was dying and was about to enter into the afterlife. She was watching over me while I slept, which made me feel so comforted and safe. I began to rub my eyes in disbelief, but to my delight she continued to bless me with her angelic presence. As I looked into her eyes, I could feel the pureness of her gaze, then she faded and I drifted blissfully, back to sleep.

Have you ever felt a gentle tickling sensation? It may have been the wings of an Angel brushing softly against you. I believe that Angels guide and protect each and every one of us. They are constantly communicating their messages to us, as explained in Doreen Virtue's book *Messages from Your Angels, What your Angels Want You to Know.*

Have you ever been in a situation where you thought you must have had a guardian Angel by your side? You most likely did — Angels surround and protect us all the time. They are here to help us fulfill our hopes and desires. Pay attention to their messages by looking for the signs. You may see little sparkles of light, a colored mist or an aura. The one I find most fascinating is when they appear in the form of clouds shaped like Angel wings. We can get so preoccupied with the routine of life that we forget to connect with that higher place. Simply speak to them and invite them into your life. If you stay open to hearing the messages, you will surely have a story to share.

I had my first encounter with Archangel Michael, just after the occurrence with the Native American elder. I was in Glastonbury at the time. Archangel Michael appeared to me and I received some healing from his vibrant blue and purple light. He showed me how to use these colors to assist in healing others and also for myself. I was guided to assist someone with healing by spreading this vibrant energy into their leg, helping to relieve the pain they were suffering due to an accident.

Many years later, during a workshop, I had another interaction with Archangel Michael. I asked for his guidance and then wrote down any messages he had for me. I could feel his grand presence enter the room. My whole body started to feel strange, like I was being anesthetized. I felt totally numb. I couldn't even hold my pen, my fingers became so stiff that it fell away and my hand was immobilized — it was as if he was trying to take the pen from me.

Then Archangel Michael began speaking to me, 'You do not need to write anything down; you must be fully present and feel this experience.'

His voice was loud and clear. This occurrence was so profound that tears began to stream down my face. He showed me a sparkling golden star and placed it right in front of me. He told me all about this astral body.

He said, 'Look directly into its shimmering light—really see the pure essence of it.'

I started to examine it more closely and when I looked into the brilliant star, I felt as if I was looking into a mirror at myself. I began beaming so beautifully and so very bright that my whole body was glowing. The more I gazed into the star, the greater the sensation of exhilaration that rushed through my body. Suddenly, I saw the word GUILT staring at me, like it was on a huge billboard. I started feeling remorseful for shining so luminously—for being my true self. On some level, I was not giving myself permission to shine and this was preventing me from living my truth to the fullest potential. I was so very grateful to Archangel Michael for this moving encounter, which helped me to progress on my path to fulfilling my life's purpose.

Afterwards, the woman sitting next to me looked at my face with amazement and said, 'Wow, what happened to you? You look ten years younger.'

I actually did feel ten years younger, *and* ten pounds lighter.

The following year, I connected with him again. On this occasion, he wanted me to write down his words.

He brought me this message: 'You must surrender. It is time to let go of your fear of what other people think about you. It is also time to stop judging yourself. You must shine your light. Your purpose is to radiate luminescence for others, but make sure you keep your feet firmly on the ground.'

I followed his advice and took a closer look at myself.

You too can call upon Archangel Michael to help you in many areas of your life—to see the truth within yourself, to increase your self-esteem, and to find your life purpose. We are all glittering stars with so much illumination inside of us. At times we may forget just how much brilliance we carry. Take another deep look inside of yourself. Are you ready to shine your brightest light?

We are all curious about death and the afterlife. Let's face it— we are all going to die sometime. During a Shamanic training course that I attended, I was asked to go out into nature and find something that would represent death. At first I was looking to find an old shriveled leaf, but instead I was led to the most beautiful pink blossom I had ever seen. This flower was on the grass and separate from the other fallen blossoms from the tree. I was told that this was my teacher of death. I sat quietly and started to connect with the flower as though it was starting to come to life.

The pink was to show me of love—unconditional love. There were beautiful raindrops on it, which showed me that it was constantly being nurtured. I saw a star in the middle of the blossom, which told me that the pretty flower was at one with everything. I then saw a seed in the center and it looked just like a fetus. The dewdrops were feeding and nurturing the fetus. I was told that it would never ever go thirsty.

The feeling that had come over me from this experience was so overwhelming that it brought tears to my eyes. I was shown in this teaching of the beauty of death and not the fear associated with dying, like the old withered leaf that I had expected to find. Most importantly, I asked where the blossom wanted to be returned to, so I took it back towards the tree that it had fallen from. What was so incredible was that when I did return the flower, it had more beauty, more life and a brighter shine to it than any of the other blossoms that were still on the tree. The others weren't as vibrant or alive. On returning the beautiful blossom, I thanked it for its teachings. From that day on, my concept of death had changed. It was clear to me that nothing ever really dies. No matter where we go, there is always a connection. Like a tiny thread that never ends, we are all entwined in it, with all the different vibrant colors of the Universe.

I believe that our departed loved ones can also be our Angels, guiding and protecting us on our life's journey. I lost my best friend, Mandy, in 2002 and I was devastated. One day, soon after she passed, I was grieving from her departure and I missed her terribly—so much so, that I had a strong desire to speak with her and I really wanted to give my friend a cuddle. I told her this and I prayed and prayed for her to come to visit me. That night, I dreamed we were reunited in a serene setting. We met in a luscious, green woodland, somewhere in the English countryside—possibly Yorkshire, where she grew up. It was a warm sunny meadow with buttercups and daisies next to a small stream that meandered through the trees. We were so happy to reconnect and see one another again that we were both smiling, euphorically. We had a long chat like we used to and then we gave each other a huge hug. This was so very healing for me. I felt that I could move forward with the grieving process, at last.

Mandy still appears in my dreams and talks to me. When I was pregnant with my youngest son, Aragorn, I was over doing things at home and at work. She came to me to tell me that I needed to slow down and get some rest. I listened to her and put my feet up for a few days.

I often feel her spirit around me and I even believe that her encouragement helped me to write this book—to keep going, when at times I was ready to give up. Mandy and I walked our Shamanic and spiritual path together and when she departed this earth, a part of me no longer wanted to continue on my journey to enlightenment. However, her presence, her words and her constant support have helped me to keep going along my sacred passage. I honor her always and feel so very blessed to have her watching over me as my guardian Angel, throughout my life.

I believe that all our departed loved ones guide, heal and protect us. It is helpful to speak to them, as they are always listening (even if you do not think they are). You can try making contact by praying to them. Your nearest and dearest will try to help you as much as they are able and in the best way that they can. For example, when my father-in-law first passed over, he was trying to communicate, to Andy and I, that he was around us. One day, he physically turned off the television whilst we were in the middle of a discussion about him—we got the message, loud and clear!

Another heart-warming story is when Keanu and I first moved back to England to be with Andy. We had just moved into a new home, the week before Christmas. I was having a problem with the lights on the Christmas tree. No matter how hard I tried, I just could not make them work. It was Keanu's bedtime, so I left the lights and got him ready for bed. I tucked him in and settled down to read him a Christmas story. He quickly fell into a deep sleep and I dosed off for ten minutes or so myself.

Whilst I was asleep, I had a dream that I saw my grandparents sitting by a canal, smiling at me. (I never had the chance to meet them and I am often sad about this, because I feel so very connected to them.) I took a closer look—as if I was zooming in on them through the lens of a camera. My grandmother was sitting on a bench with my grandfather, looking very peaceful. She was knitting a pink baby sweater. She smiled at me again, as I started to walk towards the bench. My grandmother reached out to hold my left hand and as she took it, she gently placed something sparkly on my wedding ring finger. Then everything went misty and I woke up abruptly.

I went back downstairs to the living room, where there was a delightful surprise waiting for me—the Christmas tree was all lit up so beautifully! It was as if my grandparents had fixed the lights for me to prove that the dream was real.

A few days into the new year, Andy and I went out to dinner with some friends at a Chinese restaurant. After our delicious meal, I opened up my fortune cookie and to my utter astonishment, out popped a dazzling diamond ring with the message: *Will you marry me?* in Andy's handwriting. My grandparents proved to me again, they really were my Angels.

In 2005, my niece, Lisa, tragically died before her twenty-fifth birthday. When we heard of this horrific news it was a huge shock to all of us. Later on the same day, I felt her presence. I immediately knew that she was at peace, when I saw her in a vision—she looked like an Angel. She was dressed in white and had a restful aura. Lisa smiled at me, which confirmed that she was indeed happy in her new surroundings. This made the mourning much easier for me.

A month or so after Lisa's passing was my birthday. As a pleasant surprise for me, my family placed a musical candle on my cake. I usually dispose of birthday candles once they have been used—very rarely do I keep them. However, for some reason, I kept this one. I placed it in one of our kitchen drawers and promptly forgot about it.

Then one evening, I felt Lisa's presence in our home. I was sure that she was around us, so I started to speak to her.

Half way through I began to doubt myself, so I said to her, 'Lisa, if you are really here—if it is you trying to connect with me, then please give me a sign.'

Within about ten seconds, I heard a strange melody and I had no idea where it was coming from. I looked all around the kitchen to try and locate the source of the music that was playing.

'Oh my Goodness!' I exclaimed, as I opened the drawer to where the birthday candle was. 'It really is you.'

My eyes welled with tears of joyfulness and from that moment on, I never doubted my perception again.

We all have those moments when we just know that our departed loved ones are close by. Sometimes we let our rational mind take over, convincing ourselves that we made it up, or it just can't be possible. Please remember that not only is it possible, but that your loved ones are always near you, especially when you are thinking of them—reliving a moment you shared together. They are there with you, reminiscing that same experience. Don't second-guess your natural instinct—if you feel their presence then they are there. Take that moment of opportunity to talk with them—they hear you and they want you to hear them. Call upon all those dear souls you have lost and bear in mind that just because you may not be able to see them, it does not mean they are not there. They want to be remembered. Honor them and most importantly keep their spirit alive. Light a candle for them, sing or play a song for them. You may wish to find their favorite flower and give it to them as an offering, by placing it next to their photograph, or on their resting place, or by just offering it back to nature. Show them that they have not been forgotten as they will never forget you.

Fairies

Wings of Amber, they call me spirit dancer.
Come and play for a while, I promise to make you smile.
It is time to frolic in the enchanted garden.
Let me take you back to your childhood years,
when you had no fears.
There is magic all around you.
Open your heart and let your imagination take you there.

Can you remember back to your childhood, when it was awesome to dream? So many possibilities existed then, but as we grow older, we lose sight of that time of innocence, a time without fear, when fun was allowed. Why is it that, as adults, we neglect to be more playful? Have we really forgotten how to dream? Maybe we are so wrapped up in this crazy world of responsibilities and trying to earn a living that we simply forget to have fun. Life becomes so mundane and filled with worries. Do you remember the last time you allowed your spirit to run free? When did you stop believing?

Have you ever been so lucky as to be touched by the world of fairies? Years ago, a friend of mine told me stories of fairies and other small magical creatures. Of course, I thought it was only something that you read about in children's books. Then one day, we went for a walk through a forest in Devon, England. During my adventure through this mystical woodland, for the first time since I was a child, I felt some kind of enchantment returning to me. The trees became more vibrant and everything seemed to come alive. I did not have a care in the world and my mind was still. I focused on the beauty that was all around me. It felt as though I was in a different world and it was an entrancing one. (Mother Nature will always speak to you if you give her the chance.) By the end of the walk I noticed the strangest thing. I looked down to see that my hiking boots, which I had doubled-knotted, had come completely untied.

'How can this be?' I asked my friend.

She laughed uproariously and explained that it must have been the pixies in the forest playing a trick on me. I looked down at my shoes once more in disbelief, but from then on I started to trust in the magic all over again and I started to become more playful—inviting more fun into my life. Do you experience enough fun in *your* life?

Have you ever seen tiny glowing lights around yourself or others? Some call them fairy lights. My son and I once witnessed this amazing encounter, on a wonderful holiday in Southern Wales. There were mysterious trees, streams and even a place called 'Crystal Mountain.' We both observed beams of light through the branches and sparkling raindrops that glistened on the leaves. They flickered so brightly it made us both giggle. After our excursion, I decided that I needed to do something with my back yard.

Have you ever heard the phrase, 'If you build it they will come?'

Well that was certainly the case with me—I went on to create a charming little fairy garden. There were many pretty flowers, with lavender and lots of heather. It was awe-inspiring to feel the tranquility and to see the loveliness of my own garden that had been brought back to life. The colorful butterflies enjoyed it too, as did the fairies!

I have heard people say that they are not creative—that they could not possibly fabricate anything worthwhile. I have then witnessed those same people go on to craft magical, beautiful things. We are all capable of wonderful creations—after all, that is why we are here. Since my connection to the fairy realm, my own creativity really started to blossom. Invite the fairies into *your* world and see what happens—you may be pleasantly surprised! They are attracted to all manner of pretty flowers, crystals and stones, so a rock garden, for instance, would be a natural dwelling place where, if you are fortunate enough, fairies may be seen. They help to remind us to be more gentle and tender with others, as well as ourselves.

After the success of my fairy garden, I was guided to fashion a fairy bedroom. I totally transformed it into a colorful, fun room, filled with fairy paintings and ornaments. This helped to encourage a very alluring and peaceful atmosphere and I found myself doing more creative writing and singing in my bedroom.

You see, no matter how old we get, we still have the child within us. You never know, one day you may be surprised whilst walking through the woods. The next time you feel something tickling you, it may well be a sprinkle of fairy dust. So whether or not you believe in the enchanted world of fairies, isn't it about time you brought out your playful side? Be adventurous, it is time to let your spirit dance!

Saints

Many years ago, I had a powerful experience with Saint Anna. I was pregnant with Keanu and I kept having a brief reoccurring dream about my aunt (my mother's dear sister, who had passed away many years prior). I was going through a difficult time and had spent all of the pregnancy by myself, feeling lonely. On the third occasion of having this unclear dream, I woke up with the name Saint Anna on my mind. That very week, my mother also had a dream of her sister (the same one I was dreaming about). Her sister told her to find me a picture or statue of Saint Anna, who was protecting me during my pregnancy with Keanu. My mother was given a statue and a photo of Saint Anna and so she sent them to me in England. It was a beautiful connection for me, especially during that trying time in my life. To this day, I always respect and honor this beautiful Saint, who came into my life so unexpectedly. She has been with me ever since and I especially called upon her during my other two pregnancies with my son, Aragorn, and my daughter, Amethyst. She helped me to feel empowered and guided. Saint Anna is often invoked during pregnancy, as she is a special patron of mothers, childless women and widows. It is said that while the Saint was praying, an Angel appeared to her, to announce that she would conceive and that her child would be blessed by the entire world. Saint Anna is well respected in many countries.

I also have a strong connection with Padre Pio. He is highly admired and honored in my parents' hometown and in that whole region of Southern Italy. Padre Pio was an Italian monk who was made into a Saint. He was also known as a mystic and he is regarded as one of the most popular made-to-be Saints in modern times. The miracle working Padre Pio was also one of the most controversial Saints, as he was said to have suffered the Stigmata for fifty years. Stigmata are feelings of pain or marks on the body, in places relative to the crucifixion wounds of Christ and they appeared on the hands of Padre Pio. The earliest known case of somebody suffering from this affliction was St. Francis of Assisi in 1224. When Padre Pio died, at the age of eighty-one, in San Giovanni Rotondo, the marks had completely vanished—his skin was left without a blemish.

To this very day, my mother still has a letter from him. When she was fourteen years old she wrote to him, asking for help in healing her mother (my grandmother) from an illness.

She received a written reply from him, in Italian, saying, 'Pray with an open heart with your intention to the spirit of God, for the health of your mother. I bless you and wish you all the best.'

My mother received great comfort and reassurance when she read these words and within a short while, my grandmother made a full recovery.

The last time we were in Italy together, my mother and my niece, Lisa, visited Foggia, the place where Padre Pio stayed. Unfortunately, on this occasion, I did not get the chance to go there, but it is a pilgrimage I am looking forward to taking with my family the next time we visit my relatives in Italy.

Every summer in my mother's hometown, Marina Di Gioiosa Jonica, there is the beautiful festival of 'Madonna del Carmine.' My family and I were fortunate enough to be there in 2003. There is partying all over the town—the streets are full of music and drumming, as the villagers bring the sacred statue from the church and put her on a boat. She is then honored by taking her across the waves in a celebration. There is a procession of boats, all decorated so beautifully.

My grandmother had difficult pregnancies with all of her children and when she was pregnant with my mother she fell very ill. My grandmother went into labor before the midwife could reach her house. The church bells where the Madonna del Carmine is honored started ringing and right at that moment, my mother was born. My grandmother named my mother Carmela, honoring the Madonna del Carmine. The statue of the Madonna del Carmine depicts five children with her and it is intriguing that my mother also went on to have five children—just like her namesake.

My mother is a great storyteller and I just love hearing the old tales of her childhood, growing up in Calabria, Italy. Another incident that happened to her, which she shared with me, was when my father and she were planning to leave Italy and move to Canada. One night, she had a very vivid dream, where the virgin mother visited her. She saw an image of the blessed mother, clothed all in black, hovering just below the ceiling.

She spoke to my mother in a soft voice, 'If you leave this town...'

My mother woke up in a fright and told my grandmother, who knew that it was some kind of warning. It wasn't until many years later, that she fully understood the nature of that warning. From the moment my parents left Italy my father was never the same. Sadly, his life, the way he had known it, had ended forever, leaving him completely powerless.

My mother is a very religious woman and she prays a lot. She did a great deal of praying when she found out that someone very close to her was ill. She prayed with all her heart and soul. That evening she dreamed of the virgin mother again, only this time she saw her walking towards her front door. My mother felt very positive about this dream and knew that her friend would soon get better.

There are many Saints to be honored and respected. I truly believe that we are blessed and surrounded by many of them.

Healing With Crystals

Crystals are such an amazingly therapeutic part of the earth. Some people, like myself, also use them to assist with healing their bodies. I have experienced many healing journeys and meditations with various minerals strategically placed on and around my body. One of these was so powerful that by the time I came out of the journey, I was transformed in such a way that my teacher looked at me and commented to the whole class. She said that I was radiating an immense light—I felt as though the whole of the sun's energy was inside of me and the rays were exploding out of my body. The journey I had taken was to activate my life purpose, with the assistance of the intense healing energy, generated by the crystals.

I found myself in front of a full-length mirror—I looked at my reflection and felt terrified to step into my life purpose. The dread was so great that it shattered the mirror and as the pieces fell to the ground, they vanished, taking all the fear with them. I started to swirl through seven veils of transformation. I felt as though I was traveling through my ego—thoughts of my negative aspects suddenly became very apparent and then they shattered too, just like the mirror. These veils represented layers of myself. I started to travel through each color of my chakras. When every curtain was lifted, I stood once again in front of a mirror, only this time I saw my truth and accepted that I was ready to live my purpose, without any trepidation. It was such an awesome experience, that it had left my whole body trembling. This helped my belief in the power of crystals to grow even stronger because, a few days later, a series of synchronistic events followed and I have never looked back.

My favorite crystal has always been amethyst, so much so that I named my only daughter after the precious gem. It is a very medicinal stone for me. When I was pregnant with Amethyst, I had many complications. One of them was in my ninth week of pregnancy—she flipped over my uterus, blocking my bladder. I was in a great deal of discomfort and had to rush myself to the hospital. The doctor gave me an exercise to perform, which would hopefully return my uterus back to where it should be. I had the weekend to do this and if unsuccessful, I was due to return for sedation, so they could manipulate it back to its normal place.

I did the exercises all weekend while surrounding myself with my therapeutic amethyst cathedral stones. I placed them all around me as I meditated to ease the distress. It certainly took most of the discomfort away and by the closing stages of the weekend, with great relief, my uterus had corrected itself.

Another crystal that I love to have all over my home, especially in my office, is citrine. It is very good for attracting abundance and is one of the few stones that does not accumulate negative energy. I also like to have rose quartz crystals around me. The calming energy they bring helps to attract love, balance and harmony. Celestite is great for calling the Angels to work with you. If you are looking for a stone to ground yourself, you may want to consider black tourmaline or hematite. I carry hematite with me on long journeys, particularly on a plane, as I find it helps prevent jet lag.

Many people are becoming more attracted to crystals, introducing the mineral kingdom into their lives through beautiful jewelry and sometimes using them as ornaments throughout their homes and offices.

One of America's most famous and best-liked inventors was Thomas Edison, who lived from 1847-1931. Although best known for his work with electricity, Edison was very interested in life after death and psychic phenomena. It is said that he slept only four hours a night—thus adding ten more years to the conscious part of his life. He was fascinated with quartz crystals, and mentions them in his diary: 'Even in the formation of crystals we see a definite ordered plan at work.' Edison used crystals for creative thinking. He would visit a ranch for short vacations. In the back of the ranch, up in the hills, quartz crystal deposits could be found. Edison would hike up to the hills and dig crystals out of the pockets. He enjoyed flashing them in the sunlight, seeing the way the sun reflected on them. He would then put them in his pants pocket and walk back down to the ranch house for lunch. (It was said that he was an uncommonly big eater—he'd eat a lunch big enough for several people.) Next he would come out to the front porch and sit back, just lolling around with his hands in his pockets, fingering the crystals he had found, grinning and looking at the sky. He would see all kinds of images in the clouds, and would enter a relaxed state of reverie. These were his 'dream crystals,' and perhaps they helped him tune into the right, intuitive side of the brain. An inventor, usually, will first visualize the things he or she creates and then make what they have seen. Many inventors have said something to the effect of, 'I saw it. I don't know who invented it, but they showed it to me and I saw it, and then built what I had seen.' *Crystal Healing, The Next Step*, Phyllis Galde, Llewellyn, 1988, St.Paul, MN.

What is your favorite crystal? If you don't have one, you can usually find a good selection in any crystal or new age store. Invite some magic into your life. A great reference book describing the metaphysical properties of the Mineral Kingdom is *Love is the Earth – A Kaleidoscope of Crystals* by Melody.

My family and I simply adore crystals. We have a wonderful array throughout our home. We each have our very own collection and amass more wherever we go. I feel that the strong connection I have with crystals is associated with Atlantis. I believe that I had a previous life there and I have connected with this existence in soul journeys and meditations. The legendary

American psychic, Edgar Cayce, believed that many people living today are the reincarnations of Atlantean souls. He also considered that the Atlanteans constructed giant laser-like crystals for power plants and whenever my past life journeys take me to Atlantis, I see these huge crystal pillars.

Edgar Cayce was one of the most remarkable and mysterious men of the twentieth century. Sometimes called the 'Sleeping Prophet' or 'the Miracle Man of Virginia Beach,' he was stuck with taglines that, more often than not, reflected the sensationalistic side of his work rather than its real depth and meaning. At the core, Cayce was a Christian mystic philosopher and an intuitive healer. For the forty-three years of his adult life, he taught by delivering discourses, or by giving readings while in a prayer-induced trance. These readings would then be transcribed by a secretary or family member because he could recall nothing once the twenty to forty-five minute sessions were over. The sheer volume of Edgar Cayce's output is immense. There are some 14,306 transcripts in existence today, both in print and, since the early 1990s, electronic format. Two-thirds of his readings offer holistic recommendations for treating specific physical ailments and diseases, due to the fact that he began his career as a medical intuitive and throughout his life most of those who sought him out requested readings of medical nature; all of his biographers, in fact, provide fascinating anecdotal evidence of the success of these prescriptive readings. The remaining third of Cayce's work focused on spiritual growth, dream interpretation, ancient civilizations, reincarnation, life purpose, and the many pragmatic issues of trying to integrate body, mind, and spirit into daily life, including such everyday issues as parenting and even business practices. *The Essential Edgar Cayce*, Mark Thurston, PH. D. Tarcher Penguin, New York, 2004.

My journeys to Atlantis always bring me an inner peace and serenity and are often very empowering. I believe that they have been very beneficial in helping me bring out my hidden talents and special healing abilities. I would like to share with you one of these journeys, as it was a particularly powerful one and it helped me to honor myself and to fully understand these special gifts that I was carrying forward into this life.

I saw myself carefully descending, step by stepstep-by-step, down a golden spiral staircase. When I reached the bottom, I walked towards a doorway. As I got closer, I saw a clear crystal door. I slowly opened the door and as I passed through it, I found myself in a room with seven other colorful crystal doors. Amongst them was an emerald door that I felt particularly drawn to open. I went inside and I saw two gorgeous and very powerful, tall, clear quartz, crystal pillars and then another golden staircase. I was wearing an elegant white gown, with Amethyst stones embedded within the soft, silky fabric and I wore a rainbow colored crystal necklace. I had long, blonde, silky hair with a ruby and emerald encrusted tiara set high upon my head—I looked so radiant and full of royalty and I was stunningly beautiful. I saw myself playing a harp-like instrument and I heard more soothing, melodic music playing somewhere far off in the distance. I continued to play the instrument with such grace, whilst lions lay on each side of me, guarding and protecting me and a white owl friend, with whom I used to share wisdom through divination, perched on my right shoulder. I could see white flowers everywhere and I felt like I was in paradise. As I was coming out of the journey, I felt a strong wind, blustering all around me.

This was one of a series of past life regressions that I had taken at a time when I was ready to fully understand and embrace my own power. I knew I had revisited this particular past life, at that specific time, in order to acknowledge the gift of wisdom and insight. We all carry these gifts inside us, but it is easy to forget that all we need to do to retrieve them is to connect with that quiet place within. Many people find that playing music can help them to access that profound place. In this particular journey, I felt the wisdom surfacing even more so with every note from that charming instrument. By playing, it opened doors of creativity for me—expanding myself in ways that I never thought were possible. It also seemed to me that after experiencing this particular journey, more abundance and good fortune flowed into my life. Perhaps it was because of my strong focus and desire to move forward.

Step Eight to Finding Your Life Purpose ~ Aspiration

Now take a moment for introspection. Be silent, close your eyes and take a deep breath. Call upon an Angel, Fairy, Saint or even a departed loved one. Whoever is meant to connect with you will come through. Invite them into your life to help you focus on what you desire and assist you in getting there. Be aware of all of your senses. Take in another deep breath as you become aware of who it is and feel the essence of them all around you. Feel the love that they have for you.

CHAPTER NINE

Keeping Your Dreams Alive ~ The Tree of Life and Abundance

We are one of a million stars that shine so brightly.
We all set off a spark to inspire one another.

I arose this morning with the most incredible feeling of inner peace. I had not wanted to wake up from the beautiful, tranquil dream I was enjoying:

With deep, intriguing eyes, his presence was god-like—it was he! He sat in a meditative position and was dressed all in white. His eyes pierced through my whole being, as if trying to awaken a part of me that had lain dormant. I could feel myself becoming more aware of my surroundings, as if I had finally regained consciousness, after being in a coma for many long years. The Avatar that I have known my whole life had entered my dream state, at last. He revealed his very essence and existence to me and yet, at the same time, acknowledged me for who I am.

'Me? Well, who was I?' I thought to myself.

He looked right through my eyes, as if he was unlocking the mysteries of my soul. He nodded slowly and I knew that our meeting was prearranged—it was time. I was ready to reveal myself and acknowledge who I am and what I am here to do.

I was surrounded by the sweet aroma of pretty wisteria flowers, which beautifully decorated my path. I casually walked over to smell the vibrant shrubs and I enjoyed taking the time to do so. (It is something so simple and yet so easily forgotten in our busy, everyday lives.) They were hanging down over the place where the Avatar was sitting. I felt that he was giving me a strong message—to enjoy life and the simple things around us, which we frequently overlook or take for granted.

I continued to walk towards a tree—this wasn't any old tree, it was most vigorous and quite different from any other that I had ever seen. It seemed to be more real to me.

Then I heard a voice softly whisper, 'This is the Tree of Life.'

I knew a little about this, but I did not really know its significance. I had heard that different cultures have various symbols and definitions for it, but until now, I had personally, never looked into it.

This powerful tree was like a road rising upwards, with many colossal branches, extended from the earth and reaching high into the heavens. There was also a bright light emanating from the trunk, like it was an entrance to another realm.

'Maybe this is a portal into the lower world, for my Shamanic journeying,' I wondered.

(The tree actually represented the link between Heaven and Earth.) The entrance channeled the energy flowing inside the tree and extended it up through the branches, into the sky.

I walked peacefully around this abundant and mystical creation in a sacred manner, as if it was some kind of ritual. I wanted to investigate it further—to see what I could learn from it. I caressed the branches and I immediately felt the enormity of its knowledge and wisdom shimmering through my body, touching every part of me. I knew that this tree had a wealth of information to share and would change me profoundly. It would be my teacher for life.

Since waking up from that dream, I have never been the same. My state of love, peace, beauty, enlightenment and how I interpret everything, was instantly very different from before and I was able to continue my quest with renewed vigor. We each have our mission in life to fulfill. Some of us are more aware than others and are already silently living their purpose.

The Tree Of Life

The 'Tree of Life' means many things to me: Heaven and Earth, abundance, wisdom and it is a bringer of Life, in all forms. It also represents my deep connection to other worlds, especially when I am journeying. I did some research and found that countless cultures honor the Tree of Life and have different meanings for it. A common theme is that it is a giver of gifts and spiritual wisdom. Many varieties of this tree appear in fiction and folklore and quite often it relates to fertility or immortality. The Tree of Life is both masculine and feminine, with its roots deep down in the earth and branches reaching high into the sky. It symbolizes union— having feminine sustenance and a visibly masculine form. The Tree of Life is featured in many religions, because of its potency.

According to ancient Babylonian mythology, it had magical properties and grew in the heart of paradise, where primeval rivers flowed out of its roots. The oldest known depiction of this tree is a rock carving from ancient mesopotamia. It was highly regarded by Hindus, Buddhists and other faiths, who believed it was the Peepal, Ashwatha or Bhodi Tree—in fact, at one time, every temple in India had a Peepal tree in the grounds and Buddha received his enlightenment whilst meditating under a Bodhi tree. The Greek God, Adonis, is said to have been delivered from a tree. His gift to us mortals was the strength of the powerful trunk. The Roman God, Attis, gave his spirit to the Pine tree. This later became the maypole, which started the Festival of Joy on Mid-Summer's Day. The participants celebrate by joining in with the weaving of the world, where the pole becomes the earth's axis. In Taoist tradition, immortality is bestowed by consuming a divine peach, which is produced once every three thousand years by a sacred tree. Whereas in ancient Persia it was the fruit of the White Haoma Tree that bore this gift. The ancient Sumerian God,

Dammuzi was portrayed as a tree. In Celtic tradition it was known as 'Crann Bethadh.' The Mayas believed its branches supported the heavens and referred to it as 'Yaxche.' Other traditions consider The Cebia Tree to be the world's axis. The Ancient Egyptians believed that a Holy Sycamore Tree could be found at the gateway between life and death, joining the two realms. In Norse mythology, the branches of a sacred Ash Tree, called 'Yggdrasil,' supported the abode of the Gods, whilst its roots were in the underworld.

Trees have had deep and sacred significance and played important roles in ancient mythologies and religions throughout the world. Chinese Mythology portrays a 'Tree of Life' as a phoenix and dragon, representing immortality.

The following is an excerpt from an interview on Siberian Shamanism in 1925 with the Tungus Shaman, Semyonov Semyon:

> Up above, there is a certain tree, where the souls of the Shamans are reared before they attain their powers and on the boughs of this tree are nests, in which the souls lie and are attended. The name of the tree is 'Tuuru'. The higher the nest in this tree, the stronger will the Shaman be who is raised in it, the more will he know and the farther will he see. The rim of a Shaman's drum is cut from a living Larch. The Larch is left alive, standing in recollection and honor of the tree Tuuru. At each séance, the Shaman plants a tree with one or more cross-stick, in the tent where the ceremony takes place and this tree too is called Tuuru. According to our belief, the soul of the Shaman climbs up this tree to God when he Shamanises. The tree grows during the rite and invisibly reaches the summit of heaven. *The Masks of God, Vol. 1: Primitive Mythology*, Joseph Campbell, Arkana, 1991.

In terms of Jungian psychology the World-Tree, or axis mundi, represents the personal 'meridian,' the psychological umbilical cord, which connects each individual, not only, to the divine source (realm of the Gods) but also to the vaults of the unconscious (Underworld). The quest of the mythological hero, who embarks on an adventure to search for the World-Tree, or a sacred mountain at the center of universe, is a metaphor for the quest of psychological realignment with one's own inner center and spiritual source. The task of the hero/seeker is to sublimate the cosmic energy that enters his or her being through the realignment with the 'axis mundi.' The journey is usually beset with peril and impending danger for it is a quest of transformation that requires the sacrifice of the ego. Excerpt from *The Cosmic World-Tree and The Tree of Life* by Kat Morgenstern, Sacred Earth, August, 2001.

The center, then, is pre-eminently the zone of the sacred, the zone of absolute reality. Similarly, all the other symbols of absolute reality (Trees of Life and immortality, Fountain of Youth, etc.) are also situated at the center. The road leading to the center is a 'difficult road' (durohana), and this is verified at every level of reality: difficult convolutions of a temple (as at Borobudur); pilgrimage to sacred places (like Mecca, Hardwar, Jerusalem); danger ridden voyages of the heroic expeditions in search of the Golden Fleece, the Golden Apples, the Herb of Life; wanderings in labyrinths; difficulties of the seeker for the road to the self, to the 'center' of his being, and so on. The road is arduous, fraught with perils, because it is, in fact, a rite of passage from the profane to the sacred, from the ephemeral and illusory to reality and eternity, from death to life, from man to the divinity. Attaining the center is equivalent to a consecration, an initiation; yesterday's profane and illusory existence gives place to a new, to a life that is real, enduring, and effective. *Myth Of Eternal Return*, Mircea Eliade, Princeton University Press, second paperback addition, 2005, Princeton, New Jersey

I began to recall when I was a child and what I wanted to be when I grew up. I remembered my years at school and the person I was back then.

I asked myself, 'What were my values and where did I want to take my life?'

If we look back and reconnect to those times and acknowledge the desires, hopes and dreams, how different are they today? Are they still there? Have you given up on them, because you do not believe that they are still possible? Do you think that now you are all grown up, you are no longer allowed to dream?

We should never stop dreaming or believing. If we reflect, we may find clues to what we should be doing to fulfill our life purpose. I can recollect my ninth birthday, when I received my very first diary—it was bright pink. I was so excited about this gift, because it meant that I had my own private place to express myself. There were signs from this early age that I was destined to become an author—I used to hold my pen differently than the other children. My teachers tried to get me to hold it properly, but to no avail.

I have always loved to write and over the years I have kept journal after journal, but I never pursued writing as a career when I was growing up, as I didn't think that I was smart enough. It is interesting how childhood dreams can surface again as we get older (if we allow them to). I believe that we are all capable of fulfilling our truest and deepest heart's desire. Firstly, we need to know exactly what it is that we want. We then need to find out the best way to get there. We all have different aspirations in life and some of us will get to our destination sooner than others. Just remember, it is the journey that takes us there that matters.

I had reached a point in my life where the soul searching was over. I knew what I wanted and I was looking into different ways of getting there. The road to reaching your dreams may be an easy one, whilst for some, like myself, it can be an arduous voyage, but I would not change it for anything. The world is full of miracles and is so abundant, that we are all very blessed to be here. We each have a true gift—the Gift of Life. I have learned that the more grateful I am for my existence and all of its wonders, the more beauty enters into my life. Remember to be thankful for everything that you have. Do not let your fears prevent you from attaining your goals and let go of any thought of failure. If you believe that you may fail, then you probably will. You must always stay positive.

Someone very close to me was diagnosed with a life threatening illness. He is an inspiration for me, because ever since, he has been optimistic and grateful for all that he has in his life. You would never know that he had such an affliction, as according to him, he is the master of his life, his health and his body. He chooses to be well and he has never looked better.

What inspires you in your Life? Really ask yourself this, because once you know the answer, you can build on it. Do whatever stimulates you and what makes you feel happy. Know that everything you want is within your reach and grasp for it. Most importantly, believe in yourself and keep dreaming.

I was feeling at ease, as the drumbeat lead me to my sacred willow tree. I sat with her for a while. My tree always comforts me—she is so gentle and welcoming. Whenever I meet with her, it is as if I am being cuddled. It was time for me to meet with Lia again. I was taken to the middle world, where she was waiting patiently for me.

'Hello Lia,' I said in a quiet voice.

'Hello child,' she replied. 'I have been expecting you...for I have much to say.'

We walked into an open canyon where I could see flame-colored rocks and crimson earth lay under our feet.

'Your new life is here,' she said emphatically. 'Many will think that you have changed...or that you are disconnected in some way, but for those who truly know you...they will understand your new vibration. You are no longer residing in your emotional body...yes, you are human and you will have emotion...but you are detached from the negative aspects that used to be a part of you.'

She continued to speak her words of wisdom, 'Those who are really true will not desert you...they will praise you, as they see a new person evolve. The others, who are not meant to share your growth, will abandon you...or you may feel that they have. The people, who will be in your life, are the ones who are destined to be...those who will celebrate *you* and your new ways. You are a light being...filled with love, not gloom. You have left the darkness behind you now. You have worked hard, child...I am proud of you! We will always guide you—so don't forget this...the world is yours. It is up to you to make it reality. Much beauty awaits you, as do many rewards. When you are presented with challenges...see them as a way to expand. Nobody said that life is meant to be perfect.'

I just sat there, taking it all in, as she went on, 'You will meet some wonderful people and make many new friends. As your family expands...so will your heart and your creativity. You are unique—we are all unique. Always honor and embrace your individuality. You may not yet, fully understand your potential...but as time goes by...you will.'

I made my way through the rugged bush and clambered over some red rocks, until I could see the entrance to a cave.

'Go inside, child,' Lia said.

She quickly disappeared and I realized I was going to meet with the old sorceress, once more.

'Come close, come closer, my dear, I am getting too old to stay around here. I will wait until I see you go through the gates,' she said.

'What gates?' I asked, terrified that death soon awaited me.

She cackled, 'Death! You haven't even touched that of what you came here to do. You have much work still ahead of you—this is just the beginning! You will see many things in your time and loose many close to you, my dear. You will be old and wise like me one day. I am getting ready to move on from this place, it is dark in here and I have done what I needed to do.'

Feelings of sadness flowed through me and began to fill my heart. (I was getting used to my visits in this gloomy cave with my teacher and I was not quite ready, to say goodbye.)

'I want my wisdom to be carried on by someone who can help others fulfill their lives on this planet and I have chosen you,' she explained.

'But what will I have to do and why me?' I asked, respectfully.

'It is your desire to do so,' she replied. 'You are here to teach and to inspire others, because of your pure and honest heart. Take this book,' the old woman said, as she handed it to me. 'These are ancient teachings and you now have this to take with you to many places. I will always be with you, my dear, watching and guiding you, until your time on this earth has come to an end.'

I looked at the book and I could feel my heart expanding.

'Thank you, b…but I am really confused,' I said, with a slight stutter.

'It will all make sense to you,' she replied. 'You will understand more soon, so sleep now, my dear, you have a busy dreamtime.'

After I had jotted down this journey experience, I started to write this:

You hold the key, ancient teachings of the Tree of Life. The story unfolds—the red earth is your body, your core. The blue ocean is your desire, your freedom. The rainbow is here, dreams are coming true and you are the diamond.

Much time passed by. So many positive things were starting to happen in my life and I was forever in a state of gratitude. My relationship with my husband was also growing stronger. There had been a few rough years, but we somehow managed to keep our marriage solid. We had three wonderful children, Keanu, our Indigo boy, our son, Aragorn, a crystal child and our beautiful little crystal/rainbow daughter, Amethyst. I was getting to a place where, for the first time ever, I was really comfortable with the person I was and even more comfortable with the person that I was becoming. My journeys and meditations were getting more powerful and my moments of enlightenment were becoming more frequent. These feelings were also lasting longer than they used to and there was a tranquil place, deep within my being. Perhaps this awareness had come with age (I just had my fortieth birthday and I was feeling ecstatic).

Over the years, through meditations, I repeatedly saw an old Indian man with white hair. I did not know who he was, until a friend of mine showed me a photo of him. This man was an old sage. Every now and again, I would feel his presence nearby.

On one particular occasion, I was meditating and feeling very relaxed when suddenly, he appeared in the room, right in front of me. I have heard of other people encountering things like this, but at no time had it happened to me like that. It was as if I was having a near death experience, because the whole room turned white. I then felt his presence like I never had previously and the bright light began to grow even more intensely until it was blinding me. I was suddenly aware of my heart—it felt like it was about to explode and I thought I was having a heart attack! I then had a tremendous amount of inner peace flow through my body like a fast flowing river that never stops. This was a sensation I have never felt before. What I was experiencing was a pureness of power and innocence. I could see the color of my heart charka, it was a shade of emerald green and as my heart was expanding, the hue got even brighter.

I found myself in India, where he lived and I waited by a tree. Then out of the blue, the old sage appeared with me and I saw us walking together. He guided me along a trail that led to the hallowed grounds of his resting place. I then felt as if I had lived there with him and I knew that I had been there in another lifetime. I felt so much love—a kind of flawless love that I have never known before. The old man pointed his finger to show me a mountain and I was aware of my heart again, only this time there was a sharp pain and then it quickly faded. That was the first time in my life I have been close to an immense feeling of total oneness and unconditional love. I was sobbing my then, very open, heart out. I will never forget that occasion—it truly was moving.

After I had that occurrence, various connections to India have been turning up for me and many influences that seem to be pulling me there. I have not yet traveled to India, but many of my friends have done so and they told me that it transformed their lives. I know that I am meant to go there some day and that it is a pivotal place for me— it will, no doubt, be a life changing experience. However, I will be patient and bide my time. I will go when I am truly ready. Deep in my core, where the truth resides, I know that there is something significant there for me. I will wait for my calling.

Step Nine to Finding Your Life Purpose ~ Manifestation

Now take a moment for introspection. Be silent, close your eyes and take a deep breath. Clear your mind of all thoughts for a while. Now think of everything in your life that you are truly grateful for. Give thanks for all of these things and allow your heart and soul to fill with deep gratitude. Breathe it into your entire being. Think back to when you were a child—what were your dreams and desires? Have you fulfilled them? If not, then what has stopped you from fulfilling your heart's desire?

CHAPTER TEN

Looking for Signs ~ Synchronicity

There is a thin line between time and space.
Like a rainbow that explodes its vibrant colors.

Do you ever feel like the Universe is trying to get your attention? Have you ever had a series of events steering you towards something? I remember a few summers ago, I had a calling to go to South Dakota. I kept being reminded in different ways. I ignored the intuitive nudge over and over again until, one day, I was stopped in traffic and I could not believe my eyes. Talk about a crystal clear sign from the Universe! The license plate on the car in front read, South Dakota. At that very moment, I was in total alignment with the cosmos. I finally surrendered and traveled there with my family for our summer vacation. It turned out to be a very important trip for me.

We sometimes forget to listen to that quiet voice within, or that loud knock on the door. Look for the signs—they are all around us in different forms. However, we must first be willing and open to receiving the messages they hold. When you do, you will be amazed with the end result. The Universe is always helping us in one way or another. The message, or the synchronicity, may find you in different circumstances.

I continue to get signs through license plates—this is getting to be quite regular for me. It seems that a plate will show up to guide me to the next place that I need to visit, whenever I need to go there—it is quite fun. Another example of this is when I kept getting a feeling to go to California. My life was moving in a different direction and I felt a little confused about the decisions that I was making. I was stopped at a traffic signal again, when I noticed something very peculiar about the jeep that was sitting next to me—there was nobody driving it! I looked at the empty driver's seat and then I saw that it was attached to an RV and the name of the motor home that was towing it was Spirit! Then I checked out the license plate and it was from California. The message here for me was to take control of my situation, get into the drivers seat and trust that spirit is with me. My family and I went to California, which proved to be very rewarding for us. There are signs all around us, if we would just pay more attention to what is out there.

I received another blessing in my life, during a winter snowstorm. I was standing by the window, watching the fierce wind gusting the snow everywhere.

It was one of those days when I was not feeling at my best and I thought to myself, 'This is how my day seems to be going.'

Then something magical happened. The most beautiful hummingbird suddenly appeared, facing me at my window. Feelings of joy rushed through me. Even in the middle of a snowstorm, this precious bird came to remind me of its grace and strength. There are signals everywhere. Stay in tune and you will be surprised at the miraculous experiences that are waiting for you.

Synchronicity is defined as a coincidence of events that seem to be meaningfully related. Some people who have encountered near-death experiences or mystical awakenings (such as Kundalini awakenings) describe a marked rise in the amount of synchronistic events that happen to them. This is regular occurrence in the study of mystical symbol systems, like Kabbalah.

The eminent Swiss psychiatrist Carl G. Jung (1875-1961), who first coined the term synchronicity, had been developing his own views on the subject for almost thirty years and was in his mid seventies before he formally set down his thoughts, which were associated with this particular ESP phenomena. In a lecture Jung gave at the 1951 Eranos conference in Ascona,

Switzerland, he recalled a 'run' or series of incidents to do with fish, which he considered classical synchronicity or 'food for thought':

I noticed the following on April 1, 1949: Today is Friday. We have fish for lunch. Somebody happens to mention the custom of making an 'April Fish' of someone. That same morning I made a note of an inscription, which read: 'Est homo totus medius piscis ab imo.' (A man with the body of a fish.) In the afternoon a former patient of mine, whom I had not seen in months, showed me some extremely impressive pictures of fish, which she had painted in the meantime. In the evening I was shown a piece of embroidery with fish-like sea monsters in it. On the morning of April 2 another patient, whom I had not seen for many years, told me a dream in which she stood on the shore of a lake and saw a large fish that swam straight towards her and landed at her feet. I was, at this time, engaged on a study of the fish symbolism in history. Only one of the persons mentioned here knew anything about it.

As a pendant to what I have said above, I should like to mention that I wrote these lines sitting by the lake. Just as I had finished this sentence, I walked over to the sea wall and there lay a dead fish, about a foot long, apparently uninjured. No fish had been there the previous evening. (Presumably it had been pulled out of the water by a bird of prey or a cat.) The fish was the seventh in the series.

At the same conference, he spoke of what has become his best-known illustration of a synchronistic occurrence:

My example concerns a young woman patient who, in spite of efforts on both sides, proved to be psychologically inaccessible. The difficulty lay in the fact that she always knew better about everything. Her excellent education had provided her with a weapon ideally suited to this purpose, namely a highly polished Cartesian rationalism with an impeccably 'geometrical' idea of reality. After several fruitless attempts to sweeten her rationalism with a somewhat more human understanding, I had to confine myself to hope that something unexpected and irrational would turn up, something that would burst the intellectual retort into which she had sealed herself. Well, I was sitting opposite her one day, with my back to the window, listening to her flow of rhetoric. She had an impressive dream the night before, in which someone had given her a golden scarab—a costly piece of jewelry. While she was still telling me the dream, I heard something behind me gently tapping on the window. I turned round and saw that it was a fairly large flying insect that was knocking against the windowpane from the outside in an obvious effort to get into the dark room. This seemed to me very strange. I opened the window immediately and caught the insect in the air as it flew in. It was a Scarabaeid beetle, or common Rose Chafer (*Cetonia aurata* L), whose gold-green color most nearly resembles that as a golden scarab. I handed the beetle to my patient with the words, 'Here is your golden scarab.' This experience punctured the desired hole in her rationalism and broke the ice of her intellectual resistance. The treatment could now be continued with satisfactory results. Both excerpts from, *Synchronicity: An Acausal connecting Principle*, Jung C.G. Collective Works – Volume 8- 1991, London: Routledge.

His notion of synchronicity is that there is a causal principle that links events having a similar meaning by their coincidence in time rather than sequentially. He claimed that there is a synchrony between the mind and the phenomenal world of perception.
The soul speaks to us in many ways:

Modern people want to banish all doubts and uncertainties from life. In the end, their souls die of hunger because mysteries are food for the soul.

The Dean of the Cathedral of San Francisco

I was considering putting this book together, after I had spent many years of writing journals and then taken time off to raise my children. Since opening myself up fully to my life's mission, the events for my family and myself have been a series of synchronicities. I feel very privileged and I am humble for all of the blessings that I continue to experience in my life. I had arrived at a place within myself where I knew I was ready to bring this book forward. I was in Colorado and was lead to a powerful labyrinth that a friend and I had come across, up in the mountains. I sat and prayed with intention for my book. Within less than twenty-four hours, the synchronistic events started to occur.

As I walked into a New Age bookstore, a mystical old woman with wiry hair greeted me. She smiled at me with the few remaining teeth that were still grasping to her gums. She had the air of an old-fashioned fortuneteller, who would perhaps give palm or tarot readings. The room was filled with old books, statues and ornaments. The only thing that seemed missing was her large crystal ball. I could tell she was highly perceptive and I found her presence a little daunting—it was almost as if she had the power to move objects with her mind. However, at the same time, I could sense her warm heart.

'Would you like a reading?' she asked me.

'I don't, really know why I am here,' I replied, quickly. 'I just felt drawn to come into your store and I feel that you may have something for me.'

'What are you looking for?' she asked.

'Well, I have a book that I have been writing, but I don't know where to go with it. I have prayed so much for guidance that I feel like a preacher,' I answered with sincerity.

'What are you writing about?' she inquired.

I gave her a brief description of the book and she said that she could give me intuitive guidance. I was happy with that, so she ushered me into the back of the shop.

I decided to relax a little and let the magic happen. I looked at the curtains that separated the space—they had pretty butterfly designs all over them. I found this enthralling, because five minutes prior to entering the store, I had just bought myself a stunning, mounted butterfly from Peru. It had two of my favorite colors—royal blue mixed with deep purple. (The symbol of the butterfly has entered my life many times, but I have noticed it especially, before a big change or transformation would take place). I was very open to the signs and the synchronicity that was flowing.

The old mystic had a stern expression on her face. She looked deeply into my eyes and then she went into an altered state. I could feel the energy in the room, rising. She was starting to look very connected to her source. She began talking about different publishing companies and the ones that she felt would be suitable for my book. She continued by giving me advice for submitting a book proposal. (I had not even started on my proposal yet, as I had spent most of my time in Colorado praying for guidance with this, whilst on a Crystal Healing training course.)

The mystical woman then vivaciously held out a copy of *Souls Don't Lie* by Jenny Smedley. It was published by O Books, which she felt would be a good company to approach. I reached for the book with my left hand and with only the tips of my fingers touching it, suddenly this almighty, earsplitting racket, blasted the room, scaring me half to death! It was so loud and unexpected that it made me scream and my whole body jolted out of my seat. I struggled for my breath.

'What was that? What just happened?' I asked her, still gasping for what was the last of my startled air.

'That was a sign!' she exclaimed with excitement.

She picked up the object that had caused all the commotion. It was a Tibetan bell that had fallen abruptly from the ceiling, where it was hanging.

'Really?' I asked.

I was also feeling exhilarated by now—so much so that I began to cry. Tears of truth and knowing slowly trickled down my humble cheeks. At this point, I too, felt like I was entering an altered state.

'You must submit your book proposal to O Books,' said the mystic.

My body was trembling slightly and I was getting a little freaked out, as everything seemed to be happening at a lightening fast pace. I thought of the parking meter and how I ought to get back to my car, before I got a ticket.

'Thank you so much,' I said to the medium. 'I'll see you later.'

I hurried outside and put some more coins into the meter, before crossing the street towards a hotel, where I felt sure there would be a public restroom. I began to question what had just happened and I asked the Creator to show me another sign if this was all true and if I should quickly act on this information. At that very moment, strange things started to happen—it was as if the Universe was only allowing me to see what I was meant to see, like I was in a different place and time. I noticed two businessmen in suits, walking towards me. Time stood still and I was only aware of what I was being shown. The men had papers in their hands that they were discussing.

As they walked by me, I could see they were holding important documents and I heard one of them say to the other, 'Are you ready to sign the contract?'

It was like he was talking directly to me, as if someone had drowned out the noise of the busy street, so that all I could hear was his voice. I felt like I had somehow entered the 'Twilight Zone.' My rational mind took over, I thought of my friend, who I was supposed to meet in a half hour, my flight that was leaving in the morning and my ever-increasing urge to relieve myself.

Whilst I was in the washroom, I prayed to all of my helpers, teachers and Angels, 'If this really is a sign, then please show me one word, just one word, to reassure me that all of this is real.'

As I was leaving the hotel, I was drawn to go into the gift shop—I had a strong feeling there was something inside for me.

The shopkeeper asked, 'Can I help you Madame?'

The first thing that I saw was a chocolate bar with one word on it. The fancy letters jumped right out at me, with pretty colors of pink, green and purple, all on a white background with balloons and streamers. I sniggered to myself.

'No thank you,' I said to the lady. 'I got what I came in for!'

She had a very confused look on her face as I left the store. The word written on that luxurious bar of chocolate was 'Congratulations.' There was nothing in the world that could interfere with that special moment. If I had ever doubted the guidance of God before, then that very instant ensured I never would again.

I decided to extend my stay, so I could write the proposal, as I was determined to send it off before I left Colorado. To my amazement, my hotel had free international calls. I could not believe this, as I have never known any other hotel to offer this service. I thought of my dear friend Victoria, in England, who always has time to listen to other people with an open heart. I first met her when I was seven months pregnant with Keanu. She has been a mentor for me ever since, constantly offering her advice and support. I called her to explain what had just happened. She was thrilled and as usual, offered her encouragement. It just so happened that Victoria had taken some time off work and was at home. She graciously volunteered to help me work on the proposal. As I strived to bring my book to life, it turned into another journey in itself.

I needed to go away for a weekend, to get inspired to do some writing for this book. I headed to the west coast of Vancouver Island to a powerful place called Tofino, where the golden sandy beaches stretch out for miles, amongst towering rainforests. It is especially intoxicating to visit in the winter months, during the storm season. That was when I was going and I was looking forward to watching the enormous surf, pounding against the shore.

By the time I arrived it was evening and I was too tired to do any work. The next morning, I went for a walk on the beach. I was feeling clouded and could not focus my energy on the book. I was getting worried that I had come here for nothing and that I would have to go back home. I really wanted to focus my attention on my purpose for being there—getting more of my book completed. I decided to go into the town for a short while to clear my head. I love to browse around the local gift shops and admire all the fantastic First Nations artifacts. I found a place to park near the art gallery. I had no intention of going inside, I was just going to pop into my favorite store and then head back to the hotel, but for some reason, I felt strongly guided to enter the gallery. It was as if some unseen force was reeling me in. As soon as I walked through the door there was a man standing there, welcoming me into the room. I had arrived at the perfect moment, just as a well-respected, First Nations artist and storyteller had begun to speak. I smiled, as I knew that spirit had guided me here for a reason.

The elder's words were exactly what I needed to hear. He was talking about how our passage in life is like a canoe ride. We continue on our voyage and depending on how we choose to steer our canoe, we will affect others on their journey. His teachings reopened my heart and I could feel my soul speak to me once again. His words were like the huge waves that were crashing against the rocks on my morning walk. His sincerity touched my being, awakening me to remind me of my purpose.

He spoke of how we are all teachers, healers and warriors and how we all have a tale to tell. Our own story, as we ride the oceans in our canoes. The insightful man then shared a sacred gift with us—a song from his people. He said that this was a present for us to take on our blessed voyage in the canoe. He said that even if we do not remember the song, if we sing it with him, it would remain inside of our being, forever. He played out the beat on his drum, whilst all of our voices sang in harmony with one another—this divine song, given to him by his people, that he was now, graciously sharing with us. I felt so thankful to spirit and to all of the people, both alive and departed who are in my life. As I went over to show my appreciation, I told him why I had come to Tofino—that I felt blurred and was guided to come here at the perfect time.

He shook my hand, looked me in the eyes and said, 'The elders, they listened to your prayers.'

He grinned at me and I smiled back, amiably, with immense appreciation.

The Labyrinth of Your Life

What is a Labyrinth? Unlike a maze, a labyrinth has only one path, which starts from the outer edge, moves into the heart, or center (which for some is a vortex of energy) and then backs out again. Has this forgotten mystery suddenly emerged, or are we just awakening to the call of our Divine Mother? The Divine Mother is repeatedly linked with the Labyrinth—a woman who nurtures and protects us, she empowers us into the world, with courage and integrity. Based on one of the most ancient signs for Goddess, the spiral symbol contains the power and wisdom of all earth's people.

The first time I was called to a Labyrinth was back in 1993. Andy and I had been together for just over a year. We serendipitously came across mysterious Labyrinth rock carvings, whilst vacationing in Cornwall, England. I remember it being very foggy that day, which made it even more mystical. These Bronze Age, classical, seven ring Labyrinths are still very detailed and are etched into a slate rock face, which is said to weep after heavy rain. It has been suggested that this type of carving symbolizes prehistoric man's soul, journeying from death to eventual rebirth.

The Hopi people identify the Labyrinth as the symbol of Mother Earth and the center as the belly of the Goddess. The Druids had stones on which they created small Labyrinths in sand, earth or chalk, as part of rituals. The Hindus and Buddhists, especially Tibetan Buddhists, create Mandalas—sacred circle patterns usually made from colored sand, which they then destroy at the end of the ceremony. There are many kinds of Labyrinths found all over the world. The earliest recovered was incised on a clay tablet from Pylos.

Labyrinths inspire peak or mystical experiences leading to illumination, joy and oneness with the Universe. The magic of them seems to create an altered state of consciousness. Their energy is subtly affected by the weather and the seasons. Some ancients believed it to be the other way around—that Labyrinths could affect the weather. If you walk this sacred path on the Equinox or Solstice, you can tap into the energy, creating a more empowering experience. You cannot get lost in a true Labyrinth, as it has purpose, leading you on a meaningful voyage to the core—you have no choice but to look within. The heart or center is also a doorway to another realm—perhaps a gateway to your soul. Some have said that they experience a state of timelessness, or they surrender, whilst others say that walking a Labyrinth has helped them to find the sacredness within. In my experience, Labyrinths have always brought to me an inner peace—connecting me to my truth. I can't help but feel deeply connected with my essence—my soul, every time I have walked one. Labyrinths can be used as a mystical tool for the soul and they seem to awaken the divine within. Upon entering a Labyrinth—the inward journey, you may find that you want to shed some thoughts or even release your emotions, as purging may take place. It is a wonderful way to quiet your mind. When you reach the pivot, you can pray or meditate, you may even receive messages or blessings. You then make your way to the outward journey. This may help you to understand your soul's mission, as you connect with a higher power, or whatever healing forces are at work. You may even unite with the energies or receive the wisdom of the Divine Mother. If you are called to a Labyrinth, walk it with great ease and with an open heart—you may hear your very essence speak to you. When walking the Labyrinth, let your soul guide you into your own sacred pathway—the journey of your core. Listen to your own guidance in how you wish to connect with the Sacred Labyrinth—The Sacred You.

I knew that it was time to meet with my guide, Lia, again, so I took a journey to re-connect with her.

'The wind is calling…do not be scared. What is it you are afraid of?' she asked. 'Your own identity…your own power? Go with it, child...it will take you in the right direction. When you resist...that is when the confusion comes. Surrender to it. A bird does not turn back, because it is afraid of the wind. It continues on its path...no matter how blustery it is...letting the wind carry it. Do not turn your back on your destiny ...the old man does not let his providence worry him. You are protected, child. Allow your imagination to set you free...like a child playing unrestrained, with no worries. You have been on your voyage for a long time...you are on the right track. The gateway to your soul—your pure heart...will always lead you. Sometimes we forget to smile...do not take life too seriously. People get lost in the bush, but if you really know who you are...you will always find your way. There are many tomorrows in your world, but we must live for today. Fulfill your life in the moment...without looking to the future. The ancient ones will take you for initiation. Their faces may look frightening—they will paint around their eyes. This is for protection and good sight. It is how they see through people...to know their truth. Once you understand your truth...you can never go down the wrong road. Always look into the eyes...the eyes of all—that is the gateway.'

Lia began to paint her face with white circles around her eyes.

She continued, 'This is your lesson for today...the scarlet sky never fades in my world. There are no tomorrows where I live...let the red earth teach you. It will teach you well...and so will the crimson sky. The snake dance is coming soon...this is your way. Dance, child...dance.'

I was then initiated into a ceremony. My face was decorated like the others. I could still hear the drum beating through my body—I felt like I was entering into a trance. I watched my footsteps as I carefully sauntered, one step at a time. I could feel the heat of the earth under my tired feet. I was walking for what seemed like many miles. I could make out a pathway in front of me, as the road got narrower. It was becoming more visible and I could see snakes everywhere. They were dark—black and white, just like our decorated faces. The serpents made a trail for me to walk through. I was not scared of them at all—they were helping me and working with me, as I made my way through to the entrance of this new and exciting walkway. The path ahead had my colors, as if they were blended into a mystical mist, with a mixture of purple, pink and turquoise. I danced once again, with these colors of my being and my truth. I reached out my arms and moved my body, without limitation. I gracefully enthused my fingers and hands into the dance of the sacred feminine. This was such a euphoric and liberating feeling. As I continued to dance, Lia came closer to me and we danced our truth under the crimson sky.

She went on to say, 'Remember the dreams you had as a young child...the freedom you felt. I bring this memory back to you once again. Dance the same dance... dream the same dreams. Remember they are not lost...just forgotten. You can reach anything now...you have come so far in search of your truth. You have finally found yourself...the quest is over. Celebrate... celebrate yourself and your life! You must live your dream... it is time for playfulness like a fairy, child. Be free...sleep with the stars... the rainbow colors will follow you. They are you...vibrant and colorful. It is time to show the world your illumination...it is time to dance. The lessons we learn whilst here on this earth...will prepare us for our next voyage—the one that awaits us when we leave this place. The earth journey is our biggest test...so learn well, child. Then move on and take the lessons with you.'

My heart began to slow down and I could hear the call back of the drum. It was a very potent initiation and extremely empowering for me. I had to sit and compose myself for a good while, after such an adventure. I was so elated that I was filled with a sense of renewal and great ambition. I was ready for the next stage in my life.

Step Ten to Finding Your Life Purpose ~ Trust

Now take a moment for introspection. Be silent, close your eyes and take a deep breath.

Be aware of the synchronicities that are happening in your life. Trust that they are not just meaningless coincidences. Open yourself up so that you may be in total alignment with the Universe so that you can attract the positive events into your life. Invite them in with an open heart. Now with that intention, breathe in the energy.

CHAPTER ELEVEN

Reclaiming Your Power ~ A New Dawn

Tomorrow is another day.
Let the dawn awaken your eyes, eyes of a hawk
and as the night falls bring me the stars.
Ever knowing and everlasting they will remain.
Unknown to you and I, it ponders,
unlike the soul, all knowing of existence and being.

Did you ever feel that there is more to you than meets the eye? We are all mystical beings, with so much depth and capable of much more than we even realize. After many years of my inward journey, I was now ready to bring out the 'inner' me.

I asked myself, 'Why am I really here? What is my true mission? What can I do to make a difference in the world?'

The more I asked, the more messages would come to me from the Source. I recognized the signs everywhere as the pieces of the puzzle, yet again, slowly came together.

My family and I planned a trip back to England. After two years of living in Canada, we decided to re-visit the country where Andy and I had first met. I knew that before we could move on with our lives and fully embrace our new road, we needed to put a closure on some things that we had left unfinished. This trip came at a time that aligned perfectly with where I was, within myself. I knew I must finally let go of the past and step into a greater future. I suffered much heartache in England — I lost two very close friends, my Father-in-law and my beloved dog, Sparkie. They had all sadly, passed away there and I was holding on to all the lovely memories of them that I held so dear to me.

A major part of my growth happened in the years that I lived in England, but somehow, after all the soul searching, healing and transformation that I had gone through, I was still hanging on to something, not wanting to let it go—like a boat, anchored in the tide. Sometimes we find it too daunting to move on. It is easier to stick with what we know, even if it hurts us. I have heard people say that to deal with the core of it all can be overwhelming and that is the reason why many people do not attempt to look at the root of their pain. However, if we don't accept our deepest anguish or fear, then we are just digging in deeper until we drown in our emotions and eventually sink.

After visiting family and friends back in England, we were guided to explore different parts of the English countryside and visit some of the ancient power spots, such as Stonehenge and Glastonbury and then onto the rugged, windswept coastline of Cornwall. This was a huge turning point for us, because I was three months pregnant at the time, with my daughter, Amethyst, and as I became imbued with the potency of the dramatic landscape, I felt a great sense of anticipation about our future.

The energy of this pregnancy was totally different to the other two with my sons, the vibration of the gentle soul that we would name Amethyst, was nothing that I had experienced before. There was such light and vigor flowing through me that I felt excited and full of wonder. There are specific names for the new generation of children coming into the world. We already had an 'Indigo' child, my son Keanu. He carries many of the traits, such as his great sense of humor (we call him the trickster) and he is highly intuitive—he especially has very powerful dreams. His strong will has challenged Andy and I on more than one occasion and like myself, he is very perceptive. Our younger son, Aragorn is considered a 'Crystal' child and like my other children, he is one of my greatest teachers, demonstrating to me all about unconditional love. With his huge heart and super sensitivity, he will look straight into your very soul with his penetrating, big brown eyes. At three years old, Aragorn had already shown signs of being extremely psychic. Several of my guides had told me that the child I was now carrying and ushering into the world was a 'Crystal-Rainbow' girl. This made the adventure even more powerful for me, as I sensed that her sweet rejuvenating aura was assisting in our family's progression to better things.

'It is time to move on,' I kept telling myself. 'I am almost there—almost ready to embrace the future.'

(Even though it was still a little unnerving).

'What am I so scared of? What are we all scared of?' I asked myself.

We all carry fears in one form or another. There is always some kind of trepidation—we are afraid of the dark and at the same time, afraid of the light. It was time to dive deep—deep down into the ocean of my soul, where the truth resides. The truth about who I really am, not this timid little girl that I had been for most of my life. I was ready to go out into the big wide world, it was time to share my story with others and inspire them.

Where do our worries originate? For many of us, childhood situations have left a scar—on some, so deep we think they will never heal, but the truth is we can all be healed from whatever traumatic situation we have had to endure. For others, it might be the pressure of being a teenager, but whatever it stems from, it will likely manifest itself at a significant point in adult life, such as when we become parents. I honestly believe that nothing is too deeply rooted or too painful to deal with, for it is often from the most fragile and wounded that the brightest lights will eventually shine. When we are ready and brave enough to face our demons and break through the veil of our darkness, only then can we readily embrace our future. We must be willing to take that inward journey through the dark night of the soul, before we can emerge through the flame of our existence and rise up like the phoenix.

The raging wind and lashing rain were fairly ferocious, but that did not discourage us from revisiting Stonehenge. I have come to consider it a source of spiritual regeneration, which was very relevant, as like previous encounters here, I was visiting during a time of renewal and transformation in my life.

Stonehenge is Britain's best-known prehistoric monument. It attracts thousands of visitors each year. Many celebrate the summer solstice. All come to marvel at this truly magnificent temple dedicated to the ancient Gods. As always, there were many tourists here, but despite all of the people, my connection to the site was exceptionally potent—the unborn child I was carrying, assisting in the link. Andy and our boys were benefiting from a feeling of great exuberance, emitted by this powerful place. We were unified as a family and enjoyed many cuddles and smiles as we walked around these magical megaliths.

After Stonehenge, we made our way to Glastonbury, where we checked into a hotel for the night. I have had many interesting experiences here through the years (my first encounter with my Power Animal friend the wolf was here) and it was nice to be back again. This particular visit was a little different, as being pregnant with my daughter, I was connecting to the Goddess energy, which made it even more empowering for me. After being surrounded by masculine energy for so long, it was wonderful to be really invoking the divine feminine within me, for the first time.

The next morning, after breakfast, Andy and I took the boys for a walk up to the Glastonbury Tor.

It has been called a magic mountain, a faeries' glass hill, a spiral castle, a Grail castle, the Land of the Dead... a magnetic power-point, a crossroads of leys, a centre for Goddess fertility rituals and celebrations....

The first church on the Tor was probably of the late twelfth or early thirteenth century and was dedicated to St. Michael. *Glastonbury: Maker of Myths*, Frances Howard-Gordon, Gothic Image Publications, 1997, Glastonbury.

It was extremely windy and going up the steep steps of the narrow pathway, against the forceful wind was a real battle. It reminded me of how it feels when we do not surrender and trust the in universe. When we are not in our own power then we are opposing the natural flow of things and life becomes a struggle, as if we were a spawning salmon, swimming upstream against the current.

As we finally reached the top, the wind faded for a short while. I felt a sense of serenity once again and I found my center. I could feel Archangel Michael's energy around me, so I thanked him for supporting us and always providing his protection. My sense of his presence heightened and I felt as if I was standing at the gates of Heaven. In that moment, I really understood why I was here on this earth and what I was here to do—to teach and inspire others. I had been told of this purpose before, but this was different, this time I was really feeling and seeing it—fully aware of its manifestation. My teachers had been trying to show me for years, but I was too frightened to accept it and most importantly to live it. You see, ever since I was a child I have had a terrible fear of public speaking. I am a strong believer that everything will come in the most perfect time—when we are ready. In my situation, I now knew that I had done enough of the groundwork and was ready to share my light. We all have a light within us, some just prefer to dim it a little and others may even want to switch it off, because they are too scared of what they see. I had spent, what seemed like, an eternity running away from my truth, until I finally embraced it and now I just wanted to shout it out and shine like a beacon.

After the Tor we walked down to the beautiful and fragrant gardens of the Chalice Well.

Springs and wells, especially if they were situated close to sacred hills or mountains, were looked-to throughout pre-Christian times for their magical and life-giving properties. Ancient holy wells were usually tended by an old wise woman skilled in healing and counsel and, like an anchoress, she would live at the well. *Glastonbury: Maker of Myths*, Frances Howard-Gordon, Gothic Image Publications, 1997, Glastonbury.

Whilst the rest of the family was playing around the stream and small waterfall, I took some time out by myself to sit and meditate. I felt blessed as my best friend Mandy (who is in spirit) came to join me, whilst I soaked up the tranquility and healing that I was receiving from this peaceful place. The sound of the trickling water was very refreshing and to drink the pure, salubrious water from the Chalice Well was a Godsend for all of us.

We left Glastonbury and headed on to Cornwall, where (little did I know) something very important and exciting was waiting for me. We checked into our charming hotel room in the quaint old town of Tintagel. That evening, tired but relaxed, after so much traveling around, each of us slept right through until late morning. It was the best night's sleep that I had in years and I experienced a wonderful dream of pretty colored lights and fairies. They were dancing all around my head and giggling—I felt like a small child in a grown woman's body. They had come to remind me not to get caught up in my own seriousness and that I needed to be more playful and have more fun.

After a very hearty, full English breakfast, we decided to investigate Merlin's cave, which is underneath Tintagel Castle. It appears to be a natural cave, carved out of solid stone by the ferocity of the waves, crashing against the side of the cliff for an eon. The hike down to the cave was very exciting and our boys really enjoyed the adventure—clambering over rocks and crossing over the stream that meandered down the hillside to meet with the mighty ocean below.

The energy inside the cave was magical. I saw a purple aura

that was so bright; I was amazed that no one else could see it. Later, the children enjoyed great fun at the beach beside Merlin's Cave, so much so, that they did not want to leave. When they had finally had enough, Andy and Keanu went on to cross the wooden bridge that led up to the castle, which is built on top of a craggy cliff. The castle ruins are fascinating and the views out over the Atlantic far below are simply breathtaking. However, on this occasion, I thought I had better pass, as I had seen it before and I needed to save my stamina for the long walk back up the hill. Instead, I decided to take Aragorn into the town with me where there were many lovely shops to peruse. There was so much fairy energy around, I found it inspiring and many of the shops had gorgeous little fairy statues and pretty ornaments inside. There was still a feeling of enchantment here—a transcendental presence was in the air.

I opened the door to a lovely crystal shop and the second I stepped inside, I had already entered into an altered state. It was as if I was walking through a portal. Aragorn was sound asleep in his stroller and so I was able to take a good look around. There were many interesting artifacts and part of the store had been made into a kind of museum. The friendly shopkeeper came to greet me and I noticed that he had a mystical aura to him. He had deep eyes and when I looked into them, I could see his sincerity. We started talking about the metaphysical world and told each other about our own spiritual paths.

A while into our conversation, he said to me, 'There might be something here that you will be interested in. Wait there a moment, I'll be right back.'

My curiosity was now rising. When he returned, he was holding something in both hands. There it was, right in front of me. My eyes started to widen and I could feel a sigh of relief coming from deep within my soul.

'Try it on first, see if it fits your head,' he recommended.

I felt like Cinderella trying on the glass slipper.

'Yes, I thought so, it's just right,' he said. 'It's been sitting here in our museum for fourteen years, waiting for its rightful possessor.'

By this time I was totally speechless.

'It was made for a certain someone, at a gathering of healers and Shamans, back in 1992 and has been lying here ever since,' he explained. 'We knew that one day the true owner would come in to claim it.'

I tried it on my head once again—it was a perfect fit.

'Go look at yourself in the mirror,' he suggested.

I gazed at my reflection in an ornately carved mirror, perched high on a shelf and I saw myself wearing the most skillfully crafted crown. It had been made with perfect and pure intention. As I stared at myself in disbelief, my eyes filled with tears. It was not just any old tiara, it was a Goddess crown—it was me, my personality and I could identify with it on a deep level. It had my truth and my very essence inside, it even had a moonstone—a gem that I often work with that is very empowering for me.

After all of these years of searching, suffering and enduring many challenging tasks, finally the wonderful teachings and enormous growth that I experienced, had brought this gift of confirmation to me. That frightened little girl, Rosanna, who once had no voice, had finally grown and matured into a woman in her own right. It was in this little Cornish village that I had found the lost key to myself. I had returned here to reclaim 'me'—the one who had got lost somewhere along the road to illumination. My spirit Teachers had kindly led me back to this place and the mysterious man looked relieved that after all of these years, the crown that was resting there patiently, collecting dust, had finally been claimed.

There comes a time in our lives when we have to claim our birthright, to honor and own who we are and what we have come here to do. You must be who you were meant to be on this earth and the rest will follow. We all have greatness within us. Claim what is rightfully yours, from your core—your very essence, because you are truly a bright shining star. Find your truth and never ever give up on your dreams, because you have the power to achieve anything.

The Divine Feminine

I have spent most of my life and spiritual quest being afraid of owls. What I was really frightened of was myself—my own personal power. After many synchronistic events, regarding the appearance of owl feathers, I finally accepted and owned my feminine strength. Once I had stopped running from it, the spirit of the owl made itself known to me once more, only this time, in a huge way. The heavenly spirit of an owl gifted me two magnificent wings. I was so honored to accept, welcoming the wisdom and the guidance into my life. I often have visions of her—she visits me regularity in the dreamtime.

Her message is for all of us, 'Don't be afraid of your power, yourself—embrace it and all that you are, with great courage and let the magic begin.'

All the while, I was pregnant with my daughter, I felt huge changes within myself. I had spent over twelve years on my Shamanic journey feeling more connected with my masculine side. I was blessed with two incredible boys and had absorbed their male energies throughout those pregnancies. My son, Keanu, transformed my life—from the depths of darkness, to the blissful enlightenment of being. He brought me back on the right path to fulfill my life's mission. Whilst I was on the way with my youngest son, Aragorn, he brought me the strength of change and new beginnings, literally—we moved from England to Vancouver Island when I was seven months pregnant. I often think that Aragorn carried *me* through that difficult period. Then along came Amethyst...and for the first time ever I felt a real divine feminine energy within my being, waiting to emerge. Amethyst and her spirit have woken up this sacred, celestial energy, bringing me to a place I have never traveled before. I feel blessed to be able to connect with this Goddess energy, through guides, dreams and sacred dance.

One of my teachers, Layne Redmond, has been an inspiration for me, especially in her powerful book *When the Drummers were Women*. This stimulating book has helped me to reawaken my inner Goddess like I never have before—through the primordial frame drum. This has taken me to new depths of my soul, reconnecting me with the rhythm and techniques of playing the tambourine, that were used so long ago, in parts of the world like the Mediterranean, Egypt and Mesopotamia. This is a fresh and exciting journey for me that is just beginning and I am sure it will take me on many mystical and mysterious pathways, helping me to understand more about myself and the sacred feminine within. This deep yearning, that I have to find out everything I can about this ancient tradition, will take me to unknown terrain, on the inner and outer plane. I am so very excited to learn all about the frame drum and to expand myself to the divine Goddess ways.

In a meditation, I had an uplifting experience connecting to the divinity within. I saw myself in Babylonian times, standing barefoot on a beautiful beach, overlooking the clear and calm sea. The sand was pure white and there were many trees, abundant with exotic fruits, scattered all around me. I was wearing a sumptuous, burgundy and gold dress, which made me feel lavishly wealthy. I looked so very graceful. I was elated with such serenity. I was dancing my sacred dance, moving my fingers and hands so elegantly, whilst my body freely swayed from side to side. I then saw myself playing a very old type of tambourine and as I played, my spirit merged so naturally into the rhythm of the primeval sounds.

During my Shamanic journeys and past life regressions, I quite often connect with Power Animals that are serpents. It is interesting, because since my trip to Thailand, where I finally faced my fear of snakes, I have had a much stronger connection with them.

The poor snake is probably the most maligned and vilified creature that ever lived. And the most fascinating. It is alien to us in so many ways—it moves along in a curiously disturbing manner, seemingly as much at home underground and in water as on land. It is silent, swift, and terrifying.

The serpent has slithered through centuries of the most amazing variety of baseless human fantasies, superstitious, and projections. It probably has as much significance in Christianity, albeit negative, as it had in 'animist' religions. Its association with Eve didn't help its reputation, nor did Freud's idea that it was a phallic symbol...

The image of the serpent spiraling around the Tree of Life is associated with life-giving processes, dancing new life. In many early cultures, the word *snake* or *dragon* indicated the womb. The snake also represented the rhythmic, undulating movements of the womb during birthing—that miraculous technique, provided by Nature, so that two bodies can separate without injury to either.

Throughout the world and down through the ages, the spirit of the serpent has been a symbol of healing, initiation, rebirth, transformation, and secret knowledge—knowledge that only the body knows. The snake sheds its skin and reappears in a brilliant and youthful form, being perpetually renewed. This strange ability was seen as symbolic of the higher mystery of both physical and spiritual birth and rebirth. The snake is also life energy, instinct, and the felt body experience—the facilitator of creative healing.

On another level, the Primordial Serpent became the self-renewing symbol of the Goddess. It was not the body of the snake that was sacred but rather the energy exuded by this spiraling, coiling phenomenon that transcended its boundaries and influenced the surrounding world. It emerged from the depths and the waters and did not need feet to travel. What better symbol could there be for explaining and exploring energy—creative power—the flow that moves matter into vital form?

Sacred Women, Sacred Dance, Iris J. Stewart, Inner Traditions International, Rochester, Vermont, 2000.

In some cultures, the snake symbolized the umbilical cord, joining all humans to Mother Earth. The Great Goddess often had snakes as her familiars—sometimes twining around her sacred staff, as in ancient Crete—and they were worshipped as guardians of her mysteries of birth and regeneration. In Egyptian myth, the state of existence before creation was symbolized as Amduat, a many-coiled serpent from which Ra the Sun and all of creation arose, returning each night and being reborn every morning. In ancient Greece and India, snakes were considered to be lucky and snake-amulets were used as talismans against evil.

Past Lives and Empowerment

I have claimed back some of the essence of my being, through soul journeys, on more than one occasion. I have had the opportunity to travel to many of my past lives, enabling me to overcome fear, understand who I am and to recognize and embrace my special abilities, to bring them into my current lifetime. This past life regression in particular proved to be a huge benefit for me, because a few months after taking it, some very positive changes started to happen in my life and within myself.

I could hear strange music playing and my body started undulating with the snake, joining in with her rhythmic movements. As the snake came closer I could see it was a Cobra. Then I noticed a man wearing a white turban, playing the flute-like instrument that was inspiring the serpent to dance. I was somewhere in the desert—I could feel the intense dry heat on my body. They were both here to help me with this journey, so I continued to sway with the snake, imitating her dance, because it represented knowledge. As we made our sacred movements together, I looked her straight in the eyes and they suddenly turned into rubies. The cobra was now ready to assist me into my past life. I knew from the pyramids I could see, that I must be in Egypt. Then I saw a beautiful young woman, with silky black, shoulder-length hair, holding a solid gold staff. She was wearing a luxurious golden gown, adorned with precious gems that sparkled in the brilliant sunlight. I started to merge with her—we became one and I began to walk towards the Nile River.

I was admiring the rubies and emeralds that were imbedded around my lavish attire, when I heard a mysterious and unknown voice, 'You are the guardian of the Nile. Your task is to protect the river.'

'How am I to do this?' I asked.

'Through your vision—unlock your third eye,' came the reply.

'Own your voice and vision. Honor and respect the path you are walking.'

I could sense that I was a leader of some kind in this lifetime (something I had been reluctant to be in my current life) and I could feel the essence of who I was. At that precise moment, the staff that I was holding began to reflect the sun's rays and a shaft of glorious golden light shone directly into my third eye, cleansing and unblocking it. The light led me to a cave, where the walls were embellished with ancient hieroglyphics. At the other end of the cave I could see one of my teachers standing next to an ornate golden gate. She opened the gate for me and as I passed through it, I immediately transformed into the cobra. I slithered over to a magnificent golden box, at which point I turned back into myself again, wearing royal blue robes. I opened the box and inside was the most incredible heart shaped ruby, it was the size of my palm, glowing so intensely, as if it was on fire. I removed the ruby from the box and it instantly integrated into my heart—empowering me.

I heard the mysterious voice again, 'Focus on your third eye.'

As I did so, an emerald green light began to shine from it. I placed the emerald light in my heart and I took out the ruby and positioned it into my third eye, which was then sealed. I walked out of the cave, passed the pyramids and over towards the Sphinx. As I arrived, the most healing golden raindrops began to fall on me—enabling me even further.

I heard the voice, once more, 'Stand tall, walk proud. Remember this is who you are. Remember the gifts that you had here: freedom, joy and nobility. Bring them with you now for your own personal empowerment in your present lifetime.'

Another past life journey that deeply moved me, was one where I witnessed myself as a Native American man. I was very old and it was my time to leave the earth. I was making my way up a luscious, green, grassy hill, somewhere on the plains of North America. There were wild mustangs roaming free and down below was a cluster of tepees, which must have been my village. I was bare-chested and I noticed that I had unusually large hands and feet.

As I walked, I could sense my body deteriorating and getting weaker (at the same time as I was experiencing this journey, my actual physical body was feeling very heavy). I thought that I had let the people of the village down—feelings of guilt rushed through my being, making me feel worthless, as if I had failed them and myself. My breathing was getting heavier, as I neared the end of my life cycle.

When I reached the top of the hill, it started to rain and drop by drop, I could feel it cleansing my whole body. The next moment I saw thunder and lightening go through me—this was very empowering, although my fragile body was dying, my spirit was being electrified—re-energizing my soul. I could also see a wolf and a bear honoring and celebrating me. I felt my last few breaths of life on earth…and then faded. This signified the death of the masculine energy I had carried. The wolf began to howl and I could hear the people in the village singing and drumming—they were also celebrating my life. To my surprise, the people had truly loved and respected me—I hadn't failed them at all. They took my body and placed it on a kind of wooden stretcher. They carried me over to a big old tree and positioned my corpse high up in the branches, as an offering for the birds. As the corpse of the old man disintegrated, I saw a pink energy emanating from it—a feminine one, it was so beautiful and very much alive—it was the essence of my soul to be continued into the next life.

These past life journeys, along with many others, have been very beneficial to me. They have proven to be more life changing than I could ever have imagined. I am so grateful for the training I received as a past life coach with Denise Linn. Her book *Past Lives, Present Miracles* is a great resource.

My Journey of Gratitude

The end of this book was coming near and I wanted to take a journey to give thanks to my wonderful teachers, for all they had done for me, for their love, support and guidance for more than twelve years. I ended up in the lower world, where I was joined by Lia and two Australian Aboriginal men, who had white paint on their faces and bodies. I was also met by seven serpents. I seemed to be reliving the last initiation that I had with her.

'Lay down on the red earth, child,' she said.

I was being painted again, then all of a sudden, I felt myself shape-shifting into a snake and I was moving my body like the others. Lia and the two men were watching me, they appeared to be chanting, but all I could hear was the sound of a didgeridoo playing. It was getting louder and more intense and I started to move my body more quickly, in time with the rhythm. I was feeling more empowered with every movement I made. I stood up and transformed back into myself once more. I saw beautiful rainbow colors all around me and I began to dance—I was feeling so very free.

I sensed it was time to leave. As I was walking away, I stopped to say goodbye to Lia.

'We will not see each other for a while...' she told me. 'I have other guides for you, child. They will assist you during the next phase of your life.'

As she said these words, I felt a strong India and Asia connection.

'Here, child...take these blossoms...they are a symbol of our friendship—a bond that will reunite us in the afterlife.'

She was holding a bunch of yellow and white flowers, which she placed delicately in my open hands.

I spoke to her from my soul, 'Thank you for everything—for all your guidance and wisdom. You will be forever in my heart.' She replied, 'Go now, child...go live your purpose.'

I kept walking until I reached the entrance to a cave. I went inside to see the old woman, but it was very dark—she was nothing more than a shadow.

I could hear her soft voice, echoing in the cave, 'Be true to yourself, no matter what others may think.'

In front of me was a book. I could not see it, I could only feel its essence—it felt real and pure.

I began weeping uncontrollably, through my tears I called out into the darkness, 'Thank you for your insight and encouragement, I will never forget you.'

I could not see her now, but I sensed she was still there.

Eventually, I came out of the cave and the scene totally changed. It was bitterly cold, with ice and snow everywhere. I was back in the Arctic wilderness of my Inuit guides. The man and the woman came to meet me. They have been with me from the start, where it all began. They have been like mother and father to me, always nurturing, guiding and supporting me. I ran to them both and gave them the warmest embrace—I nestled my head into them, like a child safe in her parent's arms.

The kind, loving woman was knitting something. It looked like a pouch that would cover a book and it had polar bear teeth around the outside of it, for protection. They escorted me inside the igloo, but when I turned around they were gone, my Arctic wolf was standing in their place. She sat down beside me and then we were joined by the rest of the pack. We all huddled together and I felt so cozy and protected that I could easily have dosed off, but then I felt the icy cold ground beneath me and it reminded me that we need to be awake during each and every moment of our lives.

My guardians now returned and smiled at me, saying, 'You are the teacher now, it is time for you to prepare. That is why all of the wolves came here.'

We went outside to celebrate my growth and development and as we looked up to the sky, we saw the most spectacular northern lights—the aurora was dancing in celebration with us. I watched as the colors of green, blue, pink and purple, all merged together, swaying in harmony with us as we also danced. A shooting star fell from the sky and landed into my hands. It smiled at me with a twinkle and then it turned into a book.

My teachers looked at me said, 'We are very proud of how far you have traveled and that you have finally made it here with grace.'

An overwhelming feeling of joy flooded my whole being. I was also feeling very proud of myself. One at a time, they both gently reached over to kiss my forehead. It was time for my great teachers to leave.

'Thank you from the bottom of my heart and soul,' I said. 'I will miss you.'

I was now on my own, but I knew that they would always be with me in spirit—for they are a part of me. I sat quietly and continued to watch the amazing spectacle of the aurora. I felt the blessings from above, as the mystical colors started to whirl within me, I could feel the vibrant shades energizing my whole being. I thanked everyone out loud and all who were with me in my life, my teachers, my Power Animals, Angels and all who have helped me in bringing this book to life. Then there was stillness, nothing but peace and serenity and only the silence of just being present.

Your Own Journey for Gratitude

There are many things in your life for you to be grateful for. Take the time to make a list of eleven of them. Really feel each one by going through the list individually. Breathe in the love and gratitude, let it flow through your entire being, touching your very core—your soul. Now repeat the words 'Thank You', four times. Let the energy flow out of your body to the Universe. Go out into nature and give thanks to all that surrounds you. Notice the flowers, the trees and the wildlife. Study each small detail more carefully than you ever have before. Connect with their essence by breathing it in. Become one with the energy, giving thanks again for the beauty they are sharing. Feel the beauty you have inside yourself. If you are able, travel to a lake or ocean. Find yourself an inviting spot on the shore, where you can listen to the waves. Notice the rhythm of the waves as they flow towards you. Connect with each rhythmic movement of the water until you merge with their energy, becoming one with the waves and dancing with them. Give thanks and be grateful for each natural rhythm that you experience throughout your life and continue to dance with it.

Step Eleven to Finding Your Life Purpose ~ Love

Now take a moment for introspection. Be silent, close your eyes and take a deep breath.

This is all about loving yourself and reclaiming your own power with grace. Take a good look at your reflection in a full-length mirror—one that will show your whole body. Who is staring back at you? Acknowledge the person that you see. Look closely at every part of your form—your body, your facial features, your hair and anything else that is distinctive to you. Speak to that person, accept that it is you and breathe in the word 'love', as you continue to admire yourself.

Repeat to yourself seven times, 'I love you and I love everything about you.'

Now you are ready to reclaim your own power.

Inhale deeply and say, 'I am ready to reclaim my full power. I am ready to find out my mission. I am ready to listen to the wind of my soul. I am ready to fully understand and live my life purpose, with love, grace and integrity.'

Repeat this as many times as you feel necessary. Now you are ready for the next chapter of your own life. Let the magic begin.

Awakening Your Divine Soul ~ Finding Your Own Personal Empowerment

For these exercises you will require a pen, notebook or journal (you may also want to use a pencil, for sketching and maybe some different colored pens or crayons). As you go through them, write down everything that you experience. They are designed to help give you clarity of mind, body, heart and soul. By embarking on your own journey, throughout these exercises, you are making a request to yourself and to the universe to change your life in some way (if that is what you are seeking). If so, then you are truly ready. Perhaps you may like to name your Journal 'Awakening my Divine Soul' or whatever name is befitting for you. Remember to date the entries, as you will, no doubt, want to refer back to them at some point for reflection. Don't rush through the exercises, take all the time that you need. You may want to do one exercise a day, one a week or even one a month. Listen to your own guidance and do what feels right to you. Be aware of all of your senses, particularly, what you hear, see and smell whilst doing these exercises, and also how you feel. Are you conscious of any emotions that are beginning to surface? Try not to judge the experiences that you have, we are all very unique, so each individual's experiences will be quite different. Even if you don't see anything at all, just be aware of the connection that you have deep within yourself and the oneness with the whole of creation. The importance of these exercises is to awaken a part of you, so that you may hear the whispers of your soul and you can make the changes that you desire. There is no right or wrong way of doing these exercises, just be kind and true to yourself and be open to receiving the love, support and guidance from your helpers.

Eleven Exercises to Finding Your Life Purpose

Exercise One

Look deep within yourself. Who is it that you truly see? Write down four words to describe this person. Look at your outer self—examine yourself closely. Who are you? Write down four words to describe what you see from the outside. Are you happy with whom you are, both inside and out? Be completely honest with yourself. Write down everything you can about how you are feeling. Is there anything about yourself that you would like to change? If so, what is it and why?

If you would like to make changes, how best can you achieve this? Light a candle of your choice. Put out the intention to hear your truth. Speak to your soul and ask for the clearest way to understand who you truly are. Now state your intention on what you really want in your life at this present moment in time.

Exercise Two

Be adventurous. Free yourself from anything that is limiting you from truly feeling liberated. Be aware that you are on a sacred journey—your life is so very blessed. Ask yourself this: why am I here on this earth? What do I want to accomplish before I die? What are my goals? What inspires me? Write down these questions and your answers in your journal. What emotions are you experiencing? Breathe in with these emotions and feel the blessings in your life. What would your dream vacation be? Is there a special place that you have always wanted to visit? Write down four holiday destinations that you would like to go to. Start with the place that you feel most connected to and the one that excites you the most. It is a good time to plan your next trip and invite some adventure into your life.

Exercise Three

Is there any deeply rooted pain, anger, fear or guilt within your core that needs to be released? Take in a deep breath and as you breathe out, let go of any tension that is in your body. Ask yourself; is there anything you are holding on to that is ready to be released? Draw in another deep breath and go even deeper. As you breathe out, be aware of what your body is telling you and of any emotions that may surface. Ask that they be gently released. Write down the story of your life, as if you were writing a book on you, this will help you to understand where you are within yourself at this present moment. Now draw a picture that represents your life, as you see it now. Look closely at the picture, what do you see? What stands out the most? What do you like the most? Are you happy with the picture? If not, what don't you like about it? If you were to change it, what would you change? What would you change about your life?

Exercise Four

Go on a visualization journey to meet with your Power Animal. (If you prefer, you can also take a Shamanic journey with a drumming CD. There are many CDs to choose from that are widely available. Personally, I like to use the Michael Harner Shamanic drumming series, but you should use whichever one you are drawn to.) First, place your intention to meet with a Power Animal and invite this wonderful guide to meet with you in your sacred place. Close your eyes and take a deep breath, as you exhale become aware of your body—be fully present in the moment. Deep within yourself is a safe and serene place, go deeper inside to where you feel comfortable. Take another deep breath, feel your connection to the earth—imagine that you are walking on a beautiful white sandy beach. With every step that you take, become aware of the sand beneath your feet and between your toes. Now listen to the sound of the ocean. Notice your body feeling more relaxed with every wave that gently washes against the shore. You now walk to the end of the beach and reach a luscious and tropical forest. There are pretty colored flowers everywhere, breathe in their fragrance, allowing the beauty to go through your whole body. Notice the trees that are so tall and protective. When you are ready, call out for your Power Animal to show itself to you. Invite the animal to come and meet with you. What type of animal is it? How do you feel when you look at it? Ask for its name and if it has a message for you. (Don't worry if nothing appears the first time, you can always try again, even if nothing appears there may still be a message for you.) Why has this helper come to work with you? Does it have any advice for you at this time? Which area of your life has it come to help you with? Be aware of your senses. What do you see, hear or smell? What can you learn from this animal? Does it have a particular meaning for you, at this time in your life? Now feel as if you have your feet firmly planted in the earth, allowing the earth's energy to fully ground you. Take in a deep breath; wiggle your toes, feet and then the rest of your body. Be fully aware of being present now.

Come out of the meditation and draw a picture of your animal. If you didn't see an animal, take this opportunity to connect with the essence by drawing the first animal that comes to your mind. Once you have identified your Power Animal, you might like to buy a card, print or photograph of that animal as a constant reminder of its presence and guidance in your life. Give thanks to your new helper and stay connected through journeying or meditation. Remember these dear friends are here to guide you on your path.

Exercise Five

Do you have any fears in your life or about your future? As you become aware of these fears, write them down in your journal. Is there something stopping you from fulfilling the life of your dreams? Be honest with yourself and write this down. Do you have any blockages that need to be gently released? Identify these blockages. Are they stored somewhere in your body? Do a body-scan, from your feet all the way up to your head—notice which color represents each part of your body. What do these colors mean to you? Are there any that you are not comfortable with? If so, focus on those parts and the colors. What do the colors represent to you? Write down whatever comes to mind. Focus your attention on that particular part of the body and ask to gently release the energy that is stored in that area. When you are ready, replace it with a color that makes you feel good. Now draw a picture of your body using different colors for each part, as you just saw them. Write one word beside each color that associates with that part of the body. This is to help you get in touch your body and assist with shifting any stagnant energy that needs to be unblocked and released.

Write down your greatest phobias. Take another journey or meditation to meet with a spirit guide and this time ask for help in facing your greatest fears. Take in a deep breath and as you exhale, let go of all other thoughts and focus only on connecting with your guide. Call upon and invite your spirit guide to connect with you. This guide may come in the form of another animal, an Angel or sometimes a departed loved. It may even be someone you were connected to in a past life. If you would like to open up a connection to a past life, ask for guidance with this. State your intention to meet with whichever guide is assisting you at this time to help you face your fears—you may want to write this down (I always find it useful to affirm the intention first by writing it). Take another deep breath in and let go of any stress or worries that you may have. Go to that sacred place within yourself—your own sacred temple. Now go even deeper, feel every part of your body becoming more relaxed. Notice yourself walking towards a crystal clear, gently flowing river. When you reach the bank, you can see a cleansing, cascading waterfall. Walk towards it. As you get closer you can hear the sound of the free-flowing water surging into the river. Notice how connected they are—they are one, both flowing in the same direction. Stand under the waterfall and feel the therapeutic water healing you—

starting with your head, and then tickling your body as it flows down and cleanses each part of you. Draw in another deep breath, inhaling the healing energy from this magnificent waterfall. How warm or cold is the water? How does this make you feel? You notice the prismatic spray that drifts all around you. The spray disappears and you are now back on the bank, with your spirit guide before you. Who or what do you see? Is it a woman, a man, an animal or an Angel? Do you already know this guide? What do they look like? If it is a person, what are they wearing? What is their name? What guidance does your helper have for you? Ask them what message they have for you. When you have received your message, thank your new spirit guide and feel comforted in the knowledge that you can come back to this safe haven at any time to meet with them again. Now feel as if you have your feet firmly planted in the earth, allowing the earths energy to fully ground you. When you are ready, take in a deep breath, be aware of your body, and wiggle your toes, feet and then the rest of your body. Be fully aware of being present now. Now that you have come out of the meditation, what did you gain from the experience? Record all the details in your journal.

Exercise Six:

Write down everything that you know about your Mother and Father. Are you aware of any traits that you may have inherited? Are there any special skills or talents that have been passed down to you? If you have never known your biological parents, write down what you imagine them to be like. Are there any family issues that need to be forgiven? Is there something that you wanted to say, but have not been able to? If so, write a letter to your parents as a way of releasing any pain, anger, guilt, resentment or shame. If you can't bring yourself to give it to them, burn it in a sacred fire with love and light. Don't forget to state your firm intention before your begin. Next, write a letter of gratitude, giving thanks to them for all that they have given you throughout your life. Light a candle for your parents, thanking them for bringing you into this world. Honor and celebrate them for listening to your soul in asking to be born into this family.

Exercise Seven:
Is there anything else you are hanging on to that is preventing you from moving forward? Take ownership of your life and listen to your soul speak to you. Which situations have given you the most pain in your life? Bless them, give thanks for the lessons learned and then let them go. Which people caused you the most pain in your life? Bless them, give thanks for what they have taught you and then let it go. Were there any traumas in your life that you haven't healed? How has this changed you? What has come from it? How can you best transform the situation into a positive shift? Are you now ready to bring peace to this issue? If so, journey or meditate to a spirit guide to assist you with this situation, helping to bring inner serenity so you can understand it more clearly and let it go with love and light, Take a deep breath, let go of any stress that may be present. Clear your mind from any thoughts. Focus only on your breathing—the breath of life and go deeper within yourself to that safe, sacred place within your being. Take another deep breath and call upon your spirit guide to assist you. When you are comfortable and relaxed enough, visualize that you are on a beautiful, tropical beach. You can feel the warmth of the sun shining down on you. Allow the sun's rays to radiate through your entire body. Feel a calm breeze washing over you, as you ask your guide for gentle healing. You notice some dolphins playing with each other in the water. See how connected they are to one another and how at one they are with the ocean. As you connect with this therapeutic dolphin energy, invite your guide to join you. Try not to judge what or whom you see. What does your guide look like? Is it a male or female? If it is a person, what are they wearing? Now feel the oneness that you have with your guide. How do you feel when you look at your guide? Ask them

to assist you with any healing that is required in this moment. Be aware of all your senses. What steps can you take to heal the situation, to bring you more peace and serenity? Give thanks for the guidance that you have received. Notice the waves in the ocean. Move closer to them, feel their energy increasing and becoming more powerful. Inhale deeply, breathing the fresh air and allowing the energy of the ocean to rejuvenate you. As you exhale, release all the burdens you no longer want to hold on to, let it go with a big sigh of relief. As you do this, notice that the tide is ebbing, taking your unwanted baggage with it and by doing so, cleansing you. As the waves come washing back in towards you, allow them to revitalize you. Repeat this exercise with the waves seven times, remembering to breathe deeply each time. This is a wonderful exercise to release all your negativity and leaves you feeling invigorated. Now feel as if you have your feet firmly planted in the earth, allowing the earth's energy to fully ground you. When you are ready, take in a deep breath, be aware of your body, and wiggle your toes, feet and then the rest of your body. Be fully conscious of being present now. Now that you have come out of the meditation, what did you gain from the experience? Record all the details in your journal.

Exercise Eight

Invoke your Angels, Fairies or Saints. Go and get your favorite crystal, if you don't have one, ask that your guides help you to find the one that is perfect for you at this time. You can find crystals at any New Age store; many other stores have a beautiful range of crystals and gems as they are becoming more popular. Cleanse your crystal with cold water; (make sure that you can place your particular crystal into the water) you can also cleanse it by burning sage or incense around it. Light a white candle and hold your crystal in your hand. Find a quiet spot, relax and take seven deep breaths. Feel your body de-stressing and clear all thoughts from your mind. Focus on your intention to connect with a messenger. Ask who is guiding you at this moment in time. Is it an Angel or Saint? Give yourself about half an hour or so. Notice everything that is around you and be aware of how you are feeling. What message does your teacher have for you? The message may be one word, or whole sentences. Open yourself up to receiving this guidance. Invoke the Angels and Saints for miracles (I believe in miracles and have witnessed some first hand). Alternatively, if you feel drawn to the fairy realm, go outside to your garden or find an idyllic spot in nature. Bring along a piece of paper and colored crayons and draw your fairy helper. Then write down the message that is given to you. Invoke the fairies to help inspire your creativity or to help bring about change.

Give thanks to your helpers and invite them into your life to assist you on your life's journey. Remember to connect with your teachers everyday. They are ever present, guiding and protecting you. They will always be around to help you, but sometimes, you may have to remember to ask.

Exercise Nine

Bring abundance into your life by designing your own Tree of Life. Draw your tree using whatever colors you are most attracted to. Don't limit yourself and expand to express your uniqueness. Design and create your tree by allowing the energy to flow through you like a free-flowing river. You may want to add some words to it, maybe on the branches. Are there any blockages within yourself or in your life that are preventing you from having a more abundant existence? What steps can you take to attract more abundance? Be aware of what you are feeling or experiencing. You can also create your very own Tree of Life by going out into nature and bringing back something special to you (such as a branch), which can represent the Tree of Life. Design and decorate it in whatever way you want, so as when you look at it, you will be reminded of abundance and will attract more of it into your life. Use your creativity and be joyful. You may even want to go out and buy a plant, or tree and nurture this as your Tree of Life. You can also plant a nut or a seed and watch it grow into your very own tree of life. Do whatever feels right for you and don't forget to have fun with this—you are creating an abundant future.

Exercise Ten

Look for the signs in your life. Place your intention loud and clear to the Universe. You can do this by writing a letter to God or whoever is your creative source, and asking for guidance in any area of your life. Do this with pure intent; it must come from your heart and soul. You can also do this through prayer, which is something that I do a lot of. Give yourself a few days, a couple of weeks or maybe even a month. In that time, be aware of all of the signs that the Universe is giving to you, which relate to your intention. This may come in many different forms, such as a word, a person, a book or even a car license plate. Have fun with this and if you remember to stay connected with your intention, you will receive the signs. You may start to notice coincidences that follow, stay open to the synchronicities and allow the magic to flow naturally. Do everything in a sacred manner. Walk your prints on this earth in a divine way, being the best person that you can, inspiring and helping others along the way. Walk each day as if you are walking a Labyrinth. Everything is within your reach— all you need to do is believe it and grasp it! Never let go of your dreams and never stop believing in yourself. Give it all you've got, you are the best!

Exercise Eleven

Honor and Respect yourself and the sacred journey that you are on. Ask yourself this: why am I here? What is my life purpose? What do I want to accomplish in my life? What are my hopes and dreams? What empowers me? How can I make a positive change in the world? Write down these questions and the answers in your journal. Take a journey or meditation to meet with your inner child. Ask to remember the dreams you had when you were little that you haven't fulfilled yet. Take a deep breath and let go of all thoughts, worries or stress. Go to your sacred temple—that safe, quiet place within. Take another deep breath going even deeper. You are in an enchanted garden. This garden is filled with many pretty butterflies of different, vibrant colors. You can see fluffy, cuddly rabbits roaming freely amongst the wild grass. You can smell the soothing, relaxing fragrance of lavender. Take in another deep breath. You can hear the birds singing sweetly in the trees. You find yourself an inviting spot surrounded by gorgeous white, yellow and purple flowers. Now feel the union with your inner child. What do they look like? What are they wearing? What name do you give to your inner child? Ask to hear the truth and really listen to what you hear. What do you see?

When you feel that you are totally aligned with your truth, merge with it and dance your truth. Allow this reality to integrate into all that you are. Breathe in this wonderful energy. Now feel as if you have your feet firmly planted in the earth, allowing the earth's energy to fully ground you. In your own time, take in a deep breath, be aware of your body and wiggle your toes, feet and then the rest of your body. Be fully conscious of being present now. Now that you have come out of the meditation, write down everything you experienced.

When you are ready go into another meditation—this time to find your deepest light. Take a deep breath and relax your mind and body. Feel the connection that you have with your body. Wiggle your body around and then take another deep breath. Visualize your whole being, first from the inside and then be aware of your outer body. Deep within you is a beautiful white light, shimmering so brightly. Become more aware of this illumination and allow it to expand throughout your whole body. Now ask for it to shine even brighter. Focus on spreading this pure, healing energy to every part of your being. When you can see and feel this, ask your inner self, what will I do with all of this light that I carry? How can I shine out even brighter into this world? How can I fulfill my mission? How can I be of best service to others and to myself? Be aware of what your body now feels like? Do you have any ideas or inspiration regarding your life purpose? Be aware of where your thoughts are taking you. Are there any memories surfacing? Ask to fully understand what it is you are here to do. Don't judge what comes through, just let it flow naturally and stay open to all of the possibilities in your life. What would you really love to be doing on a daily basis in terms of a job or career? It is time to claim your birthright.

Lastly, ask to be shown how you can attain your full power. What steps do you now need to take in order to fully lead your life to its greatest potential? Honor and celebrate yourself and your life. Create your own unique ceremony in celebration of who you are.

Light a pretty candle, the color of your choice, then affirm, 'I celebrate and honor myself, my life and my purpose.'

Feel the love and light go through your body and then affirm, 'I am now ready to fully embrace myself and my life purpose.'

Take a deep breath in and affirm, 'I honor this purpose and I am ready to step into it, with love, light and grace.'

Be still for a while, breathe in the breath of your life and see yourself in truth. Walk your truth, be your truth and live your truth. Shine the bright light that you are. Live the best life that you can.

The Road Map to Your Life ~ Creating a Brilliant Future

Imagine that you have a crystal ball in front of you. Have you ever wondered what the future holds for you? We are all curious at some point about what the Universe has in store for us; what will we be doing in the years to come? Where will we be in our lives? Now look into the crystal ball, but instead of wondering what your life will be like, start creating it. Set your life as you want it to be. You have found your life purpose and now it's time to build on it. Move the crystal ball even closer to you, take a deep breath in, and as you exhale, release any negative thoughts about not being able to create this life.

It is never too late to start again and create a brilliant future for yourself. The only limitations are those you have set deep down in your mind. You know that anything is possible if you really put your mind to it. Why not start now. Live your purpose and create your future—the life you always dreamed of. Take another deep breath and now hold the crystal ball, bringing it up to your eyes. Look into it; see yourself having the life that you always wished for. What does it look like? Where are you living? What type of career do you have? What does it feel like to have this wonderful life? What else can you see? What else would you like to see? Focus on your breathing, whilst being aware that you are watching a preview of your life and become even more conscious of what you are seeing. Now pay attention to how you are feeling—feel the freedom, the joy, the love and the flow of abundance in all areas of your life—your good health, your wonderful relationships, the beauty of all things that surround you. Take another deep breath, breathe and inhale the feeling of having no limitations in your life. The world is yours, it is up to you to create it however you want it to be. As you breathe out, release this feeling into the world and give thanks for your wonderful life. Then ask yourself this: what steps do I need to take to create this fantastic life that I truly desire? Write down seven steps that you will take to create your exciting future.

Here are four keys to help you to create your Brilliant future:

Key One

Start off by honoring your past, it will always be a part of you—it shows where you have been and how much you have grown though your many experiences. Now let go of what haunts you or no longer serves you. Come back to the present moment and think about what you already have; build on this and then focus on the future—it is now time to make a fresh start and realize where you are going, so you can end up where you want to be. Find the best way to get there, step by step. Be patient, don't rush anything and know that everything happens in the right order and at the perfect time.

Key Two

Focus on whatever you have a passion for. What do you love doing? What comes naturally to you? What is unique about you? Pinpoint your creativity. How best can you bring this into your daily life and your career? Who do you admire and why? What do you aspire to be like and why? How does this all relate to your life? Have a clear understanding of your goals. Don't wait for someone's approval to live your purpose. Everything is within your reach—grasp for it. You are your own power supply. Have 'Soul Ccontrol' and give yourself permission to live your mission.

Key Three

What you give out into the world, you get back. Be aware of your thoughts and feelings toward others. How do you treat others? Be sure to treat them the way you would like to be treated. This will attract positive people and positive situations into your life. Focus on service—how can you best serve others? How can you best help and guide others with an open heart?

Do not let your fear paralyze you from reaching your goals. Let go of any thoughts of failure. Create only positive thoughts and focus only on positive things.

Key Four
Step into oneness with yourself, embrace life and have integrity in all that you do. Remember to have compassion for others, for our planet and for yourself. Always give thanks for everything that you have and for the wonderful people and situations that continue to come into your life. Follow your spirit and listen to your calling. Try to make a difference in the world. Take chances, but don't be reckless, capture your identity and live your truth. Experience great joy and create your own reality.

Now let's get creative. You will need some colored crayons or markers. Draw a picture of your future. Use all of the beautiful colors of the rainbow to design it. Don't think about it too much, just let it flow naturally. Take your time with this—don't be in a hurry to finish. When you have completed it, take a good look at your creation. How does it make you feel? Now take a step back and admire your masterpiece—your future. Describe it with one word. You have built it, now live it!

Now it's time to make the road map to your life. Gather together some magazines, colored crayons or markers, stickers, glue, scissors and a large, poster-size sheet of white card. Place your intention for creating a map of your future, focus on the things in your life that bring you happiness. Take a deep breath and focus your intention again on creating a brilliant future— living the life of your dreams. Bring your dreams into reality. When you look through the magazines, you will notice certain pictures or words jump right out at you. Don't question your instincts, just go with your natural flow. Cut out the pictures and words that appeal to you the most and paste them onto the sheet of card. Next, write some inspiring words of your own, using the pretty colors. Draw some designs, pictures or symbols—whatever you want to bring into your life. When you have finished, place it somewhere you can see it everyday. You can create as many of these as you like, they are fun to make and a joy to look at. I like to hang mine in my bedroom, so that I can see them before I go to bed and again when I wake up. Congratulations on creating your brilliant future. You did it!

AFTERWORD

The Greatest Teacher Is You

Grace is always present.
You imagine it is something somewhere high in the sky,
far away, and has to descend.
It is really inside you, in your heart,
and the moment you effect subsidence or merger of the mind into its
source, grace rushes forth, sprouting as from a spring within you.
Sri Ramana Maharshi

Countless people, including myself, have ventured out seeking a spiritual teacher. Many have been fortunate enough to find the perfect coach, who has helped them to find themselves and worked as a bridge, so they may cross over to the next phase of their lives and continue down the road to enlightenment. But no matter who you choose to guide you, I honestly believe the only person who can truly take you to that place deep within, is yourself. Seek as many teachers as you wish, but if you are not willing to reach into the depths of your existence, then how are you going to find out exactly who you are? You are a wonderful, mysterious creation, brought here to explore the world and yourself. Our life experience is the initiation into being. When we begin to comprehend the lessons that are presented to us, we grow and as we do so, we become closer to understanding who we are and why we are here, until one day we will come to appreciate this very thing called *life*.

You have reached the end of this book, having shared in my personal experiences and guidance. If I were to add one more thing, it would be that I wish for you to also search deep within, to find your own calling. You may be called in many different ways, but in the end the reality is, there is no greater teacher than yourself. Your soul knows all…you simply have to believe in your purpose and live it to your greatest potential.

Acknowledgements

I would first like to thank the Creator, for my life, the blessings and the magical experiences that I am forever grateful for and for all those still to come.

To my loving husband Andy Barned, for your love, patience, guidance and endurance. I so appreciate all of your hard work on the editing of the final draft of my manuscript. All of those sleepless nights and still you helped with the children. You are a wonderful father. I could never have done this without you. I am truly grateful and so very blessed to have you as my husband, soul mate and friend. I love you forever, with all my heart.

To my beloved children, Keanu, Aragorn and Amethyst. Thank you for the blessings and love that you bring to me and for shining your radiant beauty, which inspires me everyday of my life. You all bring me so much happiness. I love you all, more than words can say.

I give thanks to all of my teachers, Power Animals, Angels, Fairies and Saints for always being with me, guiding and protecting me on this mystical journey of life.

To my mother, Carmela, for your love, patience and help—caring for your grand- children—giving me the space I needed to finish this book.

To my father, Guiseppe, for the lessons I learned from you, even through your silence.

To my brother Dominic, for all of your support over the years. Especially for getting me out of that horrible basement—I am truly grateful.

I give my deepest, warmest gratitude to Denise Linn for your truth and integrity and for the incredible work that you do. I thank you for your constant guidance and support for all of us Soul Coaches. Thank you for helping me to walk through the gates of my own transformation. You inspire me everyday of my

175

life. Summerhill Ranch will stay forever in my heart.

To Victoria Sheridan, for always being there for me at the perfect time, for helping me put together my book proposal, your help with editing the first draft of the manuscript and for being a wonderful friend and mentor, always keeping me on track. I look forward to our future projects together.

To Elizabeth Bishop, thank you for that fate-filled date with destiny, which changed my life.

To Laila, my interpreter in Greenland, I give thanks to you for graciously volunteering to take me to see the wise woman and the visitor.

To Valerie Lennox for my wake-up call—critiquing on the first few chapters.

To my publisher, John Hunt, Thank you for believing in me and my book.

To everyone, both in the physical world and in spirit who contributed to bringing this book to life.

To the wise woman and the visitor in Greenland, who brought such warmth and cheer to me during our short visit together.

To everyone who has been part of my journey. Thank you for your friendship, wisdom and blessings that you brought to me.

To Lena McLean (May), my soul sister, you are a true survivor...thank you for all of your support and friendship throughout all of these years, and for all of your insightful dreams and premonitions about me...you are a true Goddess!!

To Malia, my spirit, soul sister, you inspire me with your wisdom, beauty and truth. I cannot thank you enough for the support that you gave to me during that very difficult time in my life and for the sacred time we spent together on Moloaki.

To Laila and your beautiful family for welcoming Keanu and I into your home in Hawaii and for your warm hospitality.

To Minnie McWilliams (you will never be forgotten, I honor your spirit) and Arthur Jones, for your warm welcome when Keanu and I stayed with you in Hoopa and for the wisdom that you both shared with us.

To Bruce Crouch, your warm heart and constant support is very much appreciated. You are a true friend.

To Roz Califano, my dear friend, for all of your support and guidance throughout my Shamanic and spiritual path. Thank you for reminding me to always look at the more humorous side of life.

To Curry, my dear friend, thank you for always being there for me and for healing my foot from that nasty blister, down in the canyon.

To Damon, for fulfilling our soul contract together and for the harsh reality of it. It has made me who I am today.

To Nicole for bringing humor to our adventure in Egypt and for supporting me throughout my pregnancy with Keanu.

To all my dear departed loved ones; thank you for your constant guidance. I hear you loud and clear.

To Jonathan Horwitz for introducing Shamanism into my life and for facilitating the first Shamanic workshop I ever took, which changed me forever. Thank you for being a great teacher and encouraging me to continue on my Shamanic path—it has enabled me to heal my wounds, bringing to me a different way of being, which fills my life with inner peace, balance and harmony.

To Michael Harner and all of the teachers at the Foundation for Shamanic Studies for expanding my path of Shamanism and for sharing your incredible healing techniques, which touch the hearts and change the lives of so many people in such a profound way.

To all who have kindly given me endorsements for my book. Thank you from my heart.

To Amanda Iredale, I finally did it! I love you forever, my sister, my beautiful friend.

About the Author

Rosanna Ienco is a Shamanic Practitioner, Soul Coach and Past Life Coach. Rosanna lives on Vancouver Island, British Columbia, Canada with her husband, Andy, and their three children, where she has a healing practice. Clients are drawn to her many skills — she especially helps them in understanding their life's purpose. Rosanna teaches various workshops across the globe, helping others to find personal empowerment. For more information on her workshop entitled 'Awakening your Divine Soul,' tour dates and details of the upcoming guided meditation and drumming CD visit: www.rosannaienco.com

For all other products and services, such as Soul Coaching, Soul Journeys, Soul Readings, Shamanic Healing, Past Life Coaching and Angel Readings, please visit:

www.wolvesdenhealing.com

www.divinesoulawakenings.com

www.fairytalesndcrystalmagic.com

Resources

The Foundation for Shamanic Studies
www.shamanism.org

The Scandinavian Center for Shamanic Studies
www.shamanism.dk/
Jonathan Horwitz is co-director of The Scandinavian Center for Shamanic Studies, together with Annette Høst. He regularly leads groups in England, Ireland, and continental Europe, as well as offering personal retreats at his center in southern Sweden. He has been teaching for more than 20 years and is the author of many articles on shamanism, some of which are available at www.shaman-centre.co.uk, together with information on courses, retreats, and drumming cds.

Soul Coaching: To find a Soul Coach in your area go to:
www.soul-coaching.com

Peggy McColl: www.destinies.com
Books: Your Destiny Switch
21 Distinctions of Wealth: Attract the Abundance you Deserve
CD: Magnet for Money

Book: The Way of the Shaman by Michael Harner
CD: Michael Harner's Shamanic Journey Solo and Double Drumming

Sandra Ingerman: www.sandraingerman.com
Book: Soul Retrieval: Mending the Fragmented Self
Shamanic Journeying: A Beginner's Guide
www.shamanicteachers.com

Denise Linn: www.deniselinn.com
Books: Past lives, Present Miracles
The Soul loves the Truth: Lessons learned on the path to Joy
If I can forgive so can you

Doreen Virtue: www.angeltherapy.com
Books: Messages from your Angels
Goddesses and Angels: Awakening your Inner High-Priestess and Source-eress

Anna Maria Prezio, Ph.D. : www.prezio.com
Book: Confessions of a Feng Shui Ghost-Buster
Certified Feng Shui Consultant
Radio Host, 'Spiritual Animals'
www.internetvoicesradio.com/arch-annamariaprezio.htm
'Environmental and Spiritual Reconstruction'

Jenny Smedley: www.users.globalnet.co.uk/~author/
Book: Souls Don't Lie: A True Story of Past Lives

Alessandra Belloni: www.alessandrabelloni.com
Book: Rhythm is the cure: Southern Italian Tambourine
CDs: Daughter of the Drum
Tarantata – Dance of the Ancient Spider

Layne Redmond: www.layneredmond.com
Book: When the Drummers were Women

Victoria Sheridan: Life Coaching
www.design-a-life-coaching.com
www.victoriasheridan.co.uk
www.myspiritradio.com
victoria@myspiritradio.com

Elizabeth Bishop: Book Coach
Tel: 303-440-8106

Mystic Art Medicine
Cher Lyn: Visionary Shamanic Artist
www.mysticartmedicine.com
Rolf Hicker: photography
www.hickerphoto.com

GoldenBough books
www.goldenboughbooks.com
219 North. Mt.Shasta. Blvd, California

World Wildlife Federation
www.wwf.org

Survival International
www.survival-international.org

References

Chapter One: *The Way Of the Shaman*, Michael Harner, Harper Collins, New York, Tenth anniversary edition, 1990, page 20

Chapter Seven: *Soul Retrieval, Mending the Fragmented Self*, Sandra Ingerman, Harper Collins, New York, 1991.

Chapter Eight: *Messages from Your Angels, What your Angels Want You to Know*, Doreen Virtue, Ph.D. HayHouse, Carlsbad, CA, 2002.

Chapter Eight: *The Essential Edgar Cayce*, Mark Thurston, PH. D. Tarcher Penguin, 2004, New York, pages 1 and 2.

Chapter Eight: *Crystal Healing, The Next Step*, Phyllis Galde, Llewellyn, 1988, St.Paul, MN, page 154,155

Chapter Nine: *Glastonbury Maker of Myths*, Frances Howard-Gorden, Gothic Image Publications, 1997. Glastonbury, page 9, page 65.

Chapter Nine: *The Cosmic World-Tree and The Tree of Life*, Kat Morgenstern, Sacred Earth, August, 2001,

Chapter Nine: *The Myth of the Eternal Return*, Mircea Eliade, Princeton University Press, second paperback addition, 2005, Princeton, New Jersey, page 17, page 18.

Chapter Nine: *The Masks of God, Vol. 1: Primitive Mythology*, Joseph Campbell, Arkana, 1991, page, 238.

Chapter Ten: *Synchronicity: An Acausal connecting Principle*, Jung, C.G. Collective Works – Volume 8- 1991, London: Routledge.

Chapter Ten: *The Complete Guide to Labyrinths*, Cassandra Eason, The crossing press, Berkeley, CA, 2004.

Chapter Eleven: *When The Drummers Were Women*, Layne Redmond, Three Rivers Press, New York, 1997.

Chapter Eleven: *Sacred Women, Sacred Dance*, Iris J. Stewart, Inner Traditions International, Rochester, Vermont, 2000, pages 156 and 157.

Chapter Eleven: *The Dance from Ritual to Rock and Roll—Ballet to*

Ballroom, Joost A. M. Meerloo, M.D, Philadelphia: Chilton Co, 1960.

Chapter Eleven: *The Essential Teachings of Ramana Maharshi, A Visual Journey,* edited by Matthew Greenblatt, Inner Directions Publishing, Carlsbad, California, 2003.

Cover Image copyright (2008) Rolf Hicker
www.hickerphoto.com

Mail in this

$50 Coupon

towards your purchase of

Rosanna Ienco's Teleclasses ~

11 Steps to

Finding Your Life Purpose

For more details,
information on how to redeem this coupon
and to sign up for Rosanna's free newsletter,
where your name will be entered into
a monthly draw to win a free
Life Purpose ~ Soul Reading
please visit:
www.rosannaienco.com

BOOKS

O is a symbol of the world, of oneness and unity. In different cultures it also means the "eye", symbolizing knowledge and insight. We aim to publish books that are accessible, constructive and that challenge accepted opinion, both that of academia and the "moral majority".

Our books are available in all good English language bookstores worldwide. If you don't see the book on the shelves ask the bookstore to order it for you, quoting the ISBN number and title. Alternatively you can order online (all major online retail sites carry our titles) or contact the distributor in the relevant country, listed on the copyright page.

See our website www.o-books.net for a full list of over 400 titles, growing by 100 a year.

And tune in to myspiritradio.com for our book review radio show, hosted by June-Elleni Laine, where you can listen to the authors discussing their books.

MySpiritRadio